Admiral Eddie:
The Story of America's Greatest Naval Aviator

by Edward O. M. Barry

Published by

 **köehlerbooks**™

3705 Shore Drive
Virginia Beach, VA 23455
800-435-4811
www.koehlerbooks.com

To CONNIE & ROBIN
THANK YOU FOR YOUR SERVICE!

Colorado OMXD

ADMIRAL EDDIE

The Story of
America's Greatest Naval Aviator

EDWARD O. M. BARRY

VIRGINIA BEACH
CAPE CHARLES

For Betty, Renee and Eva.
My past, my present and my future.

TABLE OF CONTENTS

INTRODUCTION

The name Edward Orrick McDonnell may not strike a chord with most Americans, but it should. Most military experts, naval historians, and aviation zealots know of the exploits and contributions of this man. Most midshipman, instructors, and professors at the United States Naval Academy at Annapolis are at least familiar with the name Eddie McDonnell, or "Eddie Mac" as he was known. There are probably several hundred other naval aviators, regular naval officers, and enlisted seaman who are aware of or knowledgeable about his contributions to the Navy in general and naval aviation in particular.

But only a few know the entire story of this American hero's humble beginnings in Baltimore, Maryland, his dramatic and meteoric rise through the ranks of the Navy, and his momentous successes in business. That is why this book is being written.

The story of my grandfather is both fascinating and tragic. Even more remarkable is that this story of his life was simply a series of tales told to me by his daughter, who is my mother, Elizabeth McDonnell Barry, or Betty.

Mom's tales allowed me to connect with the younger versions of Eddie and the amazing individuals who made up my extended family. That is why these stories are so important to me. That is why I've shared them with my wife and children. And that is why I am taking the time to write this book. I want my readers to reconnect with their past and share their memories with family members. Maybe one of them will write a book about your exploits someday. Storytelling is a way to keep our histories alive.

Seldom in life do circumstances of both fact and fiction merge better then in an oral or story tradition. Early Native Americans, as well as the ancient African tribes, had no written words, alphabets, or even letters. Their privative drawings and sketches had to be interpreted by the tribal elders and storytellers. Much, if not all, of their histories were simple life lessons repeated around campfires and in their dwellings. Yet these tales were remarkable for their accuracy and basis in fact. They relied on these oral traditions to know where and when to hunt the great herds of bison or gazelle. They relied on these stories to know where to find water on the dry plains and deserts, or locations that provided the best shelter during the cold winter months or scorching summers, which often meant the difference between life and death. That is why these oral traditions were treasured and entrusted only to the elders and leaders of their respective groups.

These stories often included the exploits of tribal leaders, war chiefs, and hunters. These tales were meant to impart life lessons and present heroic examples to future generations. How was *greatness* defined and achieved? Great battles, strategic decisions, and even blind luck were the catalysts of these often-repeated oral tales. Great leadership is often the result of following the examples of our ancestors. And these examples, or memories, are almost always imparted through the tradition of storytelling.

Such was the case in my family, a family I was adopted into. But instead of campfires and simple drawings, we had our family room, long drives, photographs, and Super 8 mm movies. I loved these times. My parents, Betty and Arthur, not only had wonderful memories, but also documented and preserved them with a huge assortment of slides, photos, and newspaper and magazine articles. I would spend hours looking through old scrapbooks and albums. When I found something new, or of interest, my parents would stop what they were doing and tell me the backstory of the picture, or why the article was written about someone with our same last name.

I was the only family member of my generation never to have known Eddie McDonnell. He died a few weeks after my birth. It was left up to Betty to tell and retell these stories to me. And while not all of my mother's stories proved to be completely correct, it is remarkable that the memories of her father were for the most part extremely accurate. It was left up to me to decide what to do with these tales. Through research and conversations with other family members and friends, I have developed a much better understanding of this complex man, Grandfather Eddie. This book is the result.

Soon after I started this process, I realized again how fortunate I was to have been adopted into this remarkable family. My childhood had been filled with love, patience, and understanding. There was always a willingness to explore, listen, and explain things to an extremely curious and precocious child. Little did I know that they were teaching me not only about life but also how to live that life to the fullest. I was truly blessed that these people were educated, wealthy, and connected. The bonus was that this group as a whole had a treasure trove of characters in their family tree. One of the most extraordinary characters was my maternal grandfather Edward Orrick McDonnell.

Being the youngest grandchild and namesake of Eddie McDonnell, it was left to my parents to regale me with tales of this remarkable hero and man. As a young child, I would imagine myself going off to war, hunting in Africa or South America, and sharing adventures with this truly extraordinary individual. I often thought how unfair it was that I didn't get to meet him. Why did my sisters and cousins get to share in his successes, know his love, and create their own memories of him, but not me?

I have recently realized, with the death of my parents, that I was left with something far more lasting and valuable than money. Admiral Edward Orrick McDonnell left me his legacy. He left me his story. This is that story. Told, retold, written, and remembered.

CHAPTER ONE

Baltimore in the 1890s was the hard, gritty industrial center of the mid-Atlantic coast. It was a working town. Soot-stained factories stood in stark contrast to the tidy immigrant neighborhoods that housed the short-lived workers and their families. The harbor was filled with ships from around the world—ships which provided everything from the bare necessities for the working class to the luxury goods that the wealthy, perched far away in their grand mansions, could desire. Just a few steps from this harbor were the rows of warehouses, as well as the bars and flop houses that catered to those hard-worn sailors, longshoreman, and laborers in search of a bit of relaxation. Violence and crime were these men's constant companions. Life was short, work was long and hard, and when they needed to blow off some steam, they knew where to go and how to get the most out of their limited time off.

It was into this world on November 13, 1891, that Edward Orrick McDonnell was born. Eddie was the youngest of Eugene and Ann Chilton McDonnell's five children and seemed bound for success and fame from birth. You see, Eddie was born with a caul, an amnion membrane that covers a baby's head at birth. According to folklore, children born with a caul are considered extremely lucky and destined for greatness. It's wonderful when these old wives' tales prove to be correct.

Eddie's mother came from a very old and distinguished pre-Revolutionary family. Her father was Dr. John Chilton of Warrenton, Virginia. He was an educated and wealthy man. He was welcomed in all the best social circles and respected among the leaders in his community. His ancestors included Lord de Chilston of Normandy. De Chilston, a senior member of William the Conqueror's staff, was a hero of the Battle of Hastings and was made a Duke upon William's ascension to the English throne. Other ancestors included three signers of the Magna Carta and numerous members of the House of Lords in the British Parliament.

Upon their arrival in the American colonies, the family continued its string of successes and wealth creation. Joseph Blackwell was a member of the Virginia House of Burgesses and a recognized leader in early government of Virginia. Captain John Chilton, also of Virginia, was a Revolutionary War hero who was killed at the battle of Brandywine. Plantation owners, merchants, doctors, and lawyers were all counted among Ann Chilton's ancestors and family.

Eddie McDonnell's father was of considerably humbler beginnings. Eugene McDonnell had emigrated as a young man from Ireland in 1858. Through hard work, tenacity, and intelligence, he became a very successful and well-known cotton exporter in the Baltimore area. He received his citizenship on December 14, 1866, in the Superior Court of Baltimore City. As my mother, Betty, would later say, "Apparently, at the Chilton home, the Irish could apply and be welcomed!"

But it was his siblings who had the greatest impact upon young Eddie. His three older brothers created the kind of environment that would challenge him to excel and mature at a rapid pace. His sister Kathleen taught him the ways of a gentleman and how to woo the fairer sex. And according to Betty, her father was a very quick study and became extremely gifted at *wooing*, even at a very young age.

But Eddie also learned as a young man that if you truly desired something, be it wealth, power, or honors, an individual would need to focus and channel all their energies toward attaining those goals.

Nothing was ever given; it must always be earned or taken. This was the life lesson that carried Eddie through some of the most dangerous and challenging achievements of the twentieth century.

As stated, Eddie's siblings had a tremendous influence on his early years. Eddie had followed his older brothers at Loyola High School in Baltimore where, despite his diminutive size, he excelled at athletics. Understanding his aptitude for science and engineering, Eddie's father sent him to the Baltimore Polytechnic Institute. His grades there were outstanding, and he graduated shortly before his seventeenth birthday.

Throughout these early years, Eddie's constant companion was his brother John, who was the closest in age and the main source of competition and camaraderie for most of his brother's life. While in their teens, they competed in swimming and lacrosse, in academics, and in vying for the attention of the young ladies of Baltimore. Later in life, the competitions became more heated and even more intense.

John would also become a successful military man. He attained the rank of brigadier general, and was in command of Floyd Bennett Field during the Second World War. John's other passions included hunting and fishing. The equal of my grandfather with a rifle or fly rod, John was Eddie's favorite companion in their later years while traveling to South America, Africa, Asia, and Alaska to hunt big game or fish for trophy salmon and trout.

Uncle John was responsible for introducing our family to the sport of English fox hunting. His home in Warrenton was in the center of the Virginia hunt country. His title was Joint Master of Fox Hounds for the local Warrenton hunt, and he was welcomed all over the country for local meets. He was the person most responsible for igniting a passion for the hunt in both my parents, as well as my aunt and godmother, Austine "Bootsie" Hearst. It was the chosen sport of my family and occupied much of my time as a child and young man. Our home in Cherry Hills Village and its stables were designed for the care of our thoroughbred hunters and entertaining other members of the Arapahoe Hunt Club.

John was also an accomplished artist and gourmet. His painting and sculptures were extraordinary, and because of his mastery of the culinary arts, an invitation to dine at his table was seldom, if ever, refused. By all accounts and measurements, he was a true renaissance man.

I was fortunate to have met my great-uncle John at my godfather Thomas Vickery's home in Baltimore, and again at his Warrenton farm when I was very young. He was over eighty, handsome, and sharp of wit, and he could still command a room. He sat ramrod straight and had the charm and presence of an old Hollywood star.

Eddie's older siblings were no less inspiring. His oldest brother, Francis, was the leader by example. He also was a naval hero during the First World War, and later a successful businessman in Baltimore. I met him for the only time later in his life. I remember an elegant man dressed in a fall tweed jacket and wearing his Loyola University school tie. Francis sat in a large red leather chair holding a glass of scotch. He was being questioned by my always curious mother, sister, and aunt. Occasionally, I would hear a burst of laughter coming from the assembled group of ladies. Francis was entertaining them with his ribald and often off-colored sense of humor. Even at eighty-six years of age, he was still charming, sharp-witted, and always a true ladies' man.

Another of the admiral's brothers was Austin. He was called Nunca by the cousins and was a brilliant scientist and researcher. I guess that being in a laboratory most of his life had caused him to become a quiet, reflective man. I didn't hear much about him, and I was never fortunate enough to meet him. My mother would tell stories of Nunca rushing home for dinner or a party still wearing his lab coat under his jacket. A true absentminded professor.

Although his daughter, Austine, called Bootsie, was my godmother, and my mother's closest cousin growing up, I never had much opportunity to discuss her father with her. But Nunca must have done something right, because his lovely daughter Bootsie would grow up to be Mrs. William Randolph Hearst Jr. and have two wonderfully successful sons, Austin and William III.

Kathleen McDonnell Vickery was the only daughter of Eugene and Ann McDonnell. With four brothers in tow, my great-aunt Kath had to be both tough and resilient. She was nicknamed "the Buffalo." Kathleen was stubborn, determined, fascinating, and the inspiration for several generations of McDonnell women. She earned the Buffalo moniker because of a trip she had taken with her nieces to Spain. My mother, my auntie Ann, my sister Kathy, and several other nieces were on that trip. All these women were considerably younger than my seventy-eight-year-old aunt Kathleen.

But, as the stories of their adventures unfolded, the one constant was always Aunt Kath. She never missed a castle or cathedral tour. Whether it was the Alhambra, the fortress at Valencia, or the streets of Barcelona, Kathleen was the catalyst and leader. The Buffalo was often up into the late evening drinking, playing backgammon, or regaling fellow travelers with tales of her family's exploits. She was enjoying the nightlife long after the younger crowd had retired. Yet, she was up at the crack of dawn, dressed and ready for any morning activity. She was always prompt and never missed out on an early adventure. Not the "Buff."

I recall that whenever my mother would speak of her aunt, she would have a smile and frequently chuckle and laugh while remembering the stories and tales of Kathleen. Her memories and recollections would often elicit the same type of response that I would get when she would speak of her father. Betty truly loved her aunt. In fact, she loved and admired her so much that she named her first child and eldest daughter Kathleen.

But this was understandable. Aunt Kathleen was truly a grand dame. Even when I met her at age eighty-two, she was still beautiful, stylish, and lit up whatever room she entered. I remember a truly statuesque lady with striking gray hair and a regal manner that commanded attention. She loved telling her inner circle that she did the best she could with the goods she got. Her best was truly remarkable.

I like to think that my own mother, Ralphine Elizabeth McDonnell

Barry, was bequeathed these traits. Betty's nerve, her grace and exuberance, along with a genuine warmth and her aristocratic bearing, were inspirational examples to all the people in her life. She truly carried on the legacy of her aunt, Eddie's sister and mentor, Kathleen McDonnell Vickery.

I mention these remarkable siblings of Eddie's because they helped shape him at an early age. They were at least partly responsible in helping him mature mentally and emotionally. His high confidence level was not found in many young men his age. Eddie's brothers and sister showed him these traits and then allowed him to become the leader he was. And of all his many strengths, everyone who knew the admiral said that his ability to inspire and lead were two of his greatest attributes.

Unfortunately, as a teenager, Eddie was both small and extremely thin. These physical impairments were causes for concern for both he and his family.

But of course, young Edward McDonnell was able to overcome these hinderances. His remarkable academic record and numerous outstanding athletic achievements were enough to convince the admissions board at Annapolis that young Eddie had all the necessary tools to excel at the United States Naval Academy.

CHAPTER TWO

S peak to anyone who attended a service academy, be it West Point, Annapolis, the Air Force Academy, or the Coast Guard Academy, and you will inevitably hear how great an effect it had on their lives. Not that everyone who attended a service academy enjoyed their time there, but the regimentation and discipline will have left an indelible mark upon the way they have thought, worked, and even lived.

Such was the case with my grandfather Eddie. The Naval Academy had truly left its mark upon young Edward McDonnell. But it was even more than that. Annapolis had a tremendous impact on my entire family. The course of several generations of McDonnell descendants was set on the day Eddie reported to the Academy.

In 1908, Annapolis was the training ground for Naval and Marine officers whose expectations were to spend their careers on combat ships of the line. Combat ships, such as destroyers, cruisers, and battleships, were for the most part the midshipmen's only choices. Certainly, there were other options such as supply, communications, or naval intelligence. But these options meant that these young adventurers would be riding a desk somewhere on shore. Those who knew Eddie knew that being a desk jockey was not an option. This young midshipman had different ideas.

Eddie was sponsored by Congressman John Gill of Maryland and entered Annapolis at age seventeen. Though only five foot six inches and one hundred and forty pounds, Eddie had dreamed of becoming a midshipman and knew that an appointment to Annapolis was critical to his future.

According to his daughter Betty, although Eddie and his family were concerned about his size, he was confident that, like his brothers before him, he would experience a growth spurt in his late teens. During his four years at the Naval Academy, through constant exercise, good nutrition, and a very healthy appetite, Eddie grew to be a husky five foot ten and weighed slightly over one hundred and eighty pounds.

One area Eddie excelled in right away at Annapolis was academics. Through a combination of superior intelligence and a tremendous work ethic, Eddie ranked at the top of his class in all areas of study. This earned him the admiration and respect of both his classmates, as well as the older midshipman.

In addition to his scholarly achievements, Eddie also gained the reputation as a bit of a ladies' man. This reputation was developed during his teen years in Baltimore, and became legendary among his fellow midshipmen due to a boxing mishap. But more on that later.

The Naval Academy also provided Eddie with the first real opportunity to develop long-term relationships, connections, and friendships that would last him a lifetime and often provide him with opportunities not afforded to non-Annapolis graduates.

One of the first great friendships Eddie developed was with a fellow named Charles Perry Mason. Charlie Mason was easygoing, slightly taller than Eddie, and athletic. Raised in Pennsylvania, Charlie was both a gentleman and a bit of a ladies' man himself. His sense of humor and almost constant smile made him the perfect foil to Eddie's much more serious manner. Eddie would often regale my mother with stories of him and Charlie out on the town or fishing and hunting on their infrequent off days and holidays.

As we'll later find out, it was Charlie Mason who followed Eddie to Naval Air Station Pensacola and there met one of the Fisher sisters, Ralphine, or Rally as she was called, the younger sister of my grandmother Helen. As fate would have it, these two academy classmates would become more than just lifelong friends. After a timely introductions and a proper courtship lasting several months, Charlie married into the Fisher family, becoming Eddie's brother-in-law.

Another member of the class of 1912 was Eddie's roommate and close friend Hugh Frazer from West Virginia. Hugh was also a scholar, athlete, and boxer. He was quite heroic and brave. These last traits earned him the Medal of Honor at the conflict in Vera Cruz, Mexico, in 1914.

The class of 1912 had many remarkable midshipmen. One of these was Richard Byrd. According to Betty, Midshipman Byrd was not well liked by many of his classmates. He was a little too brash and boastful. Much to his displeasure, he earned the nickname "Dick," which, based on my mother Betty's stories, suited this ego-driven, fame-seeking, and rather unpleasant man to a tee. Maybe it was jealousy, ego, or just the folly of youth, but Dick Byrd was held in little regard by many in the brigade at Annapolis. And for all those wondering, yes, this is the same Richard Byrd whom a few years later would claim to have flown over the North Pole. This claim was widely disputed by many, including Bernt Balchen, who accompanied Byrd as his navigator/pilot, and Dennis Rawlins, who was also closely associated with this flight. Richard Byrd was rightly awarded the Medal of Honor, whether he ever flew over or near the pole. Just the thought of risking life and limb anywhere near this isolated region, with no chance of help or rescue, must have indeed been a harrowing experience. In 1928, Byrd began his first Antarctic expedition. He achieved his goal of reaching the South Pole in November of 1929, again with his pilot/navigator Bernt Balchen.

These young men were just a few of the members of the Naval Academy class of 1912. What an extraordinary job of identifying, recruiting, and selecting these young men of high moral character, determination, and intelligence was done by the admissions staff at the Naval Academy in those years. With men like these, our enemies in the First and Second World Wars never had a chance.

My grandfather has always been described as an easygoing yet serious young man, whose calm manner and courage under fire made him extremely hard to rattle. He was able to think and react calmly to stressful and dangerous situations. His courage and gumption came from his upbringing in the rugged streets of Baltimore. Though younger and smaller than his brothers and many others his own age, Eddie was always the first in a scrap. According to his brother John, he was quite often the instigator.

These childhood trials led to Eddie becoming one of the most accomplished athletes in prep school and at the Naval Academy. In fact, prior to entering the Academy, Eddie had won medals in swimming at the Baltimore municipal games in 1907.

In 1908, boxing at Annapolis was still treated as a fitness and defensive training program for midshipmen. Yet, the importance of the boxing program at the Naval Academy cannot be underestimated. Today, it has grown into a sports tradition known as the Brigade Boxing Championships.

My grandfather was nearly undefeated and won the bronze medal as a special-weight boxing championship in his first class year. In fact, Eddie was willing to take on much larger and more experienced boxers. Eddie quickly developed a reputation as a ferocious competitor and a fearless fighter in the ring. This fearlessness led to one of his most distinguished and noticeable features, his broken nose. It was broken during an early boxing match during his first year. According to Betty, my great-uncle Charlie Mason had told her that Eddie's broken nose provided just the right amount of anger to impetuously propel Eddie to first round knockouts in that match, and in later matches, including the semi-finals that year. In addition, the broken nose made Eddie look older, tougher, manlier, and completely irresistible. This combative, warrior look was often noticed and remarked upon by females throughout Eddie's life. In fact, it was just after the broken nose match that Eddie met one of his early conquests. A young nurse at the

Academy infirmary became quite smitten with the young midshipman. His small stature and good-natured teasing seemed to have captured her eye. Although never confirmed and most definitely forbidden, this young nurse provided Eddie with many an hour of pleasant diversion from the stresses and challenges of Naval Academy life. Maybe these rumors were simply the overzealous imaginings of an adoring daughter. But based upon Eddie's future behaviors, these tales do seem quite plausible. It was also rumored that Eddie and his nurse friend remained more than just casual acquaintances for many years.

In addition to boxing, Eddie also excelled at crew. He won his crew numerals in 1910 but had to quit to more fully pursue his true passion—lacrosse.

Growing up in Maryland and playing throughout prep school gave Eddie a tremendous advantage in his chosen sport. You see, lacrosse players do not benefit from the height or weight advantages that other athletes do in sports like basketball or football. The size of the dog in the fight does not matter. Only the size of the fight in the dog matters. Speed, stealth, stick handling, and grit are the skills required to play lacrosse at the highest level. And Eddie possessed an overabundance of them all.

Eddie was originally planning on attending either Johns Hopkins or Loyola, as his older brothers had. But when Eddie's older brother Francis convinced two of his lacrosse buddies, Frank Breyer and Bill Hudgins from Johns Hopkins, to volunteer at Navy in order to help coach and mentor a team, my grandfather knew that Annapolis was the right choice.

Because freshmen were not allowed to play varsity sports at Annapolis in those years, Eddie had to wait until his second year to display his skills on the lacrosse field. And what a display it was. When Eddie started as a sophomore, he quickly became Navy's leading scorer. In fact, he led the team in scoring in each of his three years playing the attack position. In 1911, Navy hired George Finlayson as its head coach. It was Coach Finlayson who said that if they had awarded all-American honors in lacrosse at that time, Eddie would have been the first three-time unanimous winner. As it was, Eddie did earn his orange *N* in each of the years he played. Many of his teammates agreed that Eddie deserves at least part of the credit for turning the Naval Academy into a lacrosse powerhouse that has lasted to this day. Navy has won more league championships than any other school, and has won numerous national championships throughout its long and illustrious history.

As mentioned, Eddie was an outstanding student and scholar. It was his excellent grades and willingness to help others that earned him the respect of midshipman both older and younger. His leadership on the playing fields, in the ring, and in the classroom set him apart, and it was apparent that he was destined for greatness even at an early age.

But there were several areas of study in which his expertise served him well in later life. His aptitude in communications and navigation were unmatched according to Betty. Radio communication was almost unheard of in those years. Spending and receiving messages was through signal lamp flashes using Morse code. If this means of communication wasn't available, then messages were sent using flags called pinafores. This ability to send messages using pinafores proved invaluable to Eddie during the Vera Cruz campaign, as we shall learn in the coming chapter. These skills also proved extremely useful while navigating the Caribbean Sea and its numerous islands in later years. But most importantly, these skills proved to be invaluable and resulted in many lives saved, during the later parts of World War II.

Sailing was another area of study which helped determine Eddie's future as a naval aviator. The Naval Academy required that all midshipman learn to sail. They would spend several months during the summers aboard a large sailing vessel far from their home port of Annapolis. Eddie, while on these extended voyages, would spend many hours studying the shape of the sail and how it related to the creation of different air pressures on each side. These pressures propelled the sailboat much in the same way they are used to lift an aircraft. Eddie loved this part of the Academy's curriculum and realized early on that powered aircraft were going to play an important role in the Navy's arsenal in the very near future.

Powered flight was in its infancy. My grandfather had entered Annapolis in 1908. It had been only five years since the first powered flight by the Wright brothers in Kitty Hawk, North Carolina. While at the Naval Academy, Eddie had heard about and seen heavier-than-air planes and knew how important they would become to both the Navy and the Army in coming years. He knew immediately that, if offered the opportunity, he would accept and become part of this new method of waging war.

But more important than just the military aspects of these new inventions, Eddie could see many other applications for these new flying machines—transporting materials and people. Speeding up communications and travel could all be better served by incorporating aircraft. This was the future, and Eddie was slowly gaining insights into its implications. In fact, it was because of his early flight/navigation training and intimate knowledge of Central and South America developed after the First World War that Eddie was able to secure a lucrative investment banking job in the 1920s.

His skills and knowledge were vital to a new and growing industry. Commercial aviation was just beginning. Mail delivery and mapping were making huge strides once aircraft were incorporated into the process. This was why he eventually joined the active Naval Reserves and went into investment banking after World War I. He was exactly the right person, at exactly the right time, when in 1922, Grayson M-P Murphy made him an offer to join their newly launched firm. Pan American's Juan Trippe, Boeing Corporation, and United Aircraft were looking to generate capital to become viable in this new industry. But first, Eddie would graduate and begin a career that was to make him arguably the greatest naval aviator of the twentieth century.

CHAPTER THREE

E ddie graduated from the Naval Academy in June of 1912, at age twenty. It would be several months before he turned twenty-one in November of that year. He was, if not the youngest, one of the youngest men ever to graduate from Annapolis.

Upon his commissioning, young Ensign McDonnell was assigned to a variety of ships over the next two years. These included the battleships *New Jersey* and *Florida*. He also served on the cruisers *Montana* and *Montgomery* for a short time. But it was aboard the USS *Prairie* that he tasted his first true action.

The USS *Prairie* was assigned to participate in the military operations at Vera Cruz, Mexico, in 1914. I never quite understood what we were doing in Vera Cruz until recently. Apparently, just prior to the start of World War I, President Woodrow Wilson was worried about German intervention in our hemisphere and in Mexico directly. Victoriano Huerta had taken control of the Mexican government in February 1913, after a bloody coup

Ensign Edward O. McDonnell aboard the USS *Prairie*, 1914

that had initially been supported by the US Ambassador Henry L. Wilson.

About a year later, nine unarmed American sailors had "wandered" into a restricted fueling area in Tampico, Tamaulipas, Mexico. They were promptly arrested and held by the Mexican authorities. Upon their release, the US naval commander demanded an apology and a twenty-one-gun salute. The Mexican authorities complied with the apology but refused to order the salute. Woodrow Wilson requested from Congress the authorization to occupy the port of Vera Cruz in response to the slight by the Mexican government. While awaiting the occupational order, Henry Wilson, our ambassador, learned of a shipment of arms that had been routed by way of Odessa and Hamburg. They were scheduled to land in Vera Cruz around April 21, aboard the German cargo ship *Ypiranga*. In one of the great ironies, many of the weapons and much of the ammunition in this shipment was from the Remington Arms Company. It had been ordered by American financier John W. De Kay and a Russian arms dealer named Leon Rasst from Puebla, Mexico. President Wilson ordered the immediate occupation of the port of Vera Cruz with the intention of confiscating the weapons and ammunition. That was why Ensign Eddie McDonnell found himself in Vera Cruz on those fateful days in April of 1914.

The naval blockade of Vera Cruz began on April 21, under the command of Admiral Frank F. Fletcher. His opposites on the Mexican side were Generals Juan Esteban Morales and Gustavo Maass, who commanded a force of 3,360 Mexican army regulars. These troops were further reinforced by the citizens of Vera Cruz, as well as inmates from La Galera, a local military prison.

At approximately 11:12 a.m., a landing party of 500 Marines and 285-armed Navy Bluejackets under the command of William Rush left for the port. They came ashore at 11:20 and seized the railroad terminal and the cable station as ordered. A short time later, several Navy rifle companies seized the customshouse, telegraph, and post offices. Another group of Marines captured the railroad roundhouse, yard, and power plant.

The American Consul William Canada had notified Mexican General Gustavo Maass of the American's intention to occupy the port earlier that day. Maass, under orders from the Mexico City government was told not to resist or surrender. In fact, Maass was told to retreat inland approximately six miles to the city of Tejeria.

So, as the American sailors made their way toward the customshouse, they were met not by the Mexican Army regulars, but by a contingent of civilians, prisoners, and Mexican Naval Academy cadets who had not been contacted nor ordered to stand down. This mixed contingent of Mexican nationals had opened fire upon the American troops around noon.

Now, as fate would have it, Eddie was in one of the first boats to land that morning at the pier in Vera Cruz. He had been aboard the USS *Prairie,* and as a signal officer, he had been assigned to set up a communication station on shore. Ensign McDonnell, leading a small squad of Marines, had met little or no resistance on his way to his assigned station. Since most messages were delivered by pinafore flags, the squad needed to be stationed in a high, open, and exposed position so the ships in the harbor could receive the messages and direct fire at the artillery and sniper locations on shore.

Eddie accompanied his commander, William Rush, as they made their way to the Terminal Hotel. Rush had chosen this location for his onshore headquarters to be in constant communication with his superiors in the ships at anchor in the harbor. The Terminal Hotel was one of the tallest buildings in Vera Cruz, set upon a slight hill with a commanding view of the surrounding city and harbor. From the rooftop, Eddie could determine the enemy positions, fix their location, and most importantly relay that information to William Rush, as well as to the ships in the harbor. Unfortunately, Eddie and his small contingent could also be seen by the enemy combatants stationed throughout the city of Vera Cruz.

At about noon, the same time that the American troops first came under fire on their way to the customshouse, Eddie exited the door on the roof to find that a Marine who had reached it before him had been shot in the head. The Marine was severely wounded and had to be evacuated immediately. It was from this dangerous rooftop perch that Ensign McDonnell spent the next two days and nights sending and receiving messages by pinafore. He had to relay the locations of snipers and onshore artillery batteries to the gunners on board the American ships at anchor. In addition, Eddie had to keep Commander Rush advised about these locations for Rush to accurately deploy his ground forces throughout the city. My mother, Betty, still had the letter that my grandfather received from the Secretary of the Navy, Josephus Daniels, that was dated June 13, 1914. It reads,

> *To Ensign E. O. McDonnell, U. S. N., via Commander-in-Chief, Atlantic Fleet.*
>
> *Subject: Commendation—conduct with landing force at Vera Cruz, Mexico, in April, 1914*
>
> 1. *The following extract from a report of the naval operations at Vera Cruz made by Rear Admiral F. F. Fletcher is quoted for your information:*
>   *Ensign E. O. McDonnell, U. S. N., Brigade Signal Officer, posted on the roof of the Terminal Hotel and landing, established a signal station there and personally, day and night, maintaining communication between troops and ships. At this exposed post he was continually under fire. One man was killed and three wounded at his side during the 2 days' fighting. He showed extraordinary heroism and striking courage and maintained his station in the highest degree of efficiency. All signals got through, largely due to his heroic devotion to duty.*

2. *The Department highly commends the heroism and courage shown by you in maintaining your signal station in the highest degree of efficiency while under the effective fire of the enemy.*

3. *The efficiency, disregard of danger, and devotion to duty shown by you are in accord with and add to the best traditions of the Naval Service.*

4. *A copy of this letter will be made a part of your service record.*

In addition to the letter, a well-known war correspondent decided that this brash young naval officer would make a good storyline about the bloody conflict at Vera Cruz, he wrote,

Throughout the entire action there was no cooler discipline displayed than that of the signal boys who wig-wagged messages from the roof of the lofty Hotel Terminal, where they were the conspicuous mark for score of hostile riflemen. Ensign E. O. McDonnell was in command of this force.

A few marines were sent to the roof to guard the signalman. The first who stepped out into the open fell with a bullet through his head. I saw him carried on a stretcher a few minutes later into the brigade hospital in the Terminal Building. A fine stalwart young chap he was with light curling hair crowning the head that lay so still, and just below the line of the blond curls he wore 'the red badge of courage.'

In almost the same spot on this battle-swept roof another was killed while swinging his gaudy flag messages and three more were wounded. But the message scarcely faltered in the sending. As it was at Guantanamo in 1898, when the marines established Camp McCalla under a grueling fire, the flags that drooped from a stricken hand were grasped by another almost before they fell, and the story told in pantomime from the bullet-scourged parapet went on to its end. Lieutenant Howze told me that he had to send more than one hundred messages from this station, and all of them under fire, on the first day of battle. Every one of them went rough correctly and without delay. Ensign McDonnell stood through it all amid the thickest of the fire and never flinched. It was his first experience in action.

For this extraordinary courage and bravery, Eddie was awarded the Medal of Honor.

Ensign Edward Orrick McDonnell: Medal of Honor Portrait

CHAPTER FOUR

After Vera Cruz, Eddie was given an opportunity to choose which direction he wanted his naval career to take. Next to choosing Annapolis, this would be the most important decision of his young life. He could have gone to the War College and moved on to the Naval Intelligence Service, which was relatively new and would have provided him with excellent opportunities for advancement. He might have chosen a more traditional role of serving on a ship of the line and working his way up to his own command. But Eddie had something else in mind. His interest in naval aviation, fueled by his love of sailing, had started when he was in his second year at Annapolis and remained with him throughout his early years as a naval officer.

By 1910, the Navy had spent several years watching and learning about the new technologies surrounding powered flight. It had also appointed an aviation officer and hired its first pilot, a civilian name Eugene Ely who had proven that an aircraft could indeed take off from a ship. Early aviation pioneer Glenn Curtiss, knowing the Navy's interest in aviation, offered to train a Naval officer to build, maintain, and fly an aircraft at his facility in San Diego. This is how, in 1910, Lieutenant Theodore Ellyson became Naval Aviator No. 1. Ellyson's training was so thorough and complete that, less than a year later, the Navy ordered and purchased its first plane, a Curtiss A-1 Triad.

But early aviation had its share of mishaps as well. Shortly after beginning his training, Lt. Ellyson took off, and after some mechanical failures, crashed his plane in front of an airshow audience. Fortunately, he wasn't hurt badly and was able to continue his training under Curtiss.

He and Curtiss collaborated on many projects, including the basic requirements of those Navy men who wanted to become pilots. Ellyson was the first Navy man to fly at night. He was the first passenger in Curtiss's A-1 and in the new seaplane that he helped Curtiss design. Unfortunately, in 1912, Ellyson wanted to test Curtiss' newest plane, the A-2. Throwing caution into the wind, Ellyson crashed and was severely injured. After more than a month in recovery, and after testing a float plane launched from a catapult, Ellyson decided to quit flying. He was reassigned to destroyer and battleship duty until the end of World War I.

After the war, Ellyson was assigned as the executive officer at Hampton Roads' Naval Air Station in Virginia. Later, he travelled to Brazil to train their pilots. He lasted only a few months in Brazil after becoming very disenchanted by the Brazilian trainee's lack of professionalism and discipline.

Upon returning to the States, Ellyson was assigned to the USS *Lexington* to fit out the Navy's second aircraft carrier. Unfortunately, several years later, while heading home to Annapolis to be with his extremely ill daughter, his plane crashed. It was nearly two months before his body washed up on the shores of Chesapeake Bay. Early naval aviation was certainly not for the faint of heart. So, after many long hours of deliberation and discussions with those he trusted most, Eddie decided that the best path for him was in that extremely hazardous field.

Because of the dangers involved, Naval aviation training was done on a voluntary basis only. The planes were made of canvas or paper and wood. The engines had to be adapted from other types of motorized vehicles and fitted to suit the purpose. Planes were designed to take off and land on good old *terra firma*. Unfortunately, solid ground was not where the US Navy operated. How were these new flying machines going to work in a water-based environment? But as my mother told me, these were questions that her father knew he could find the answers to!

So, in the summer of 1914, Eddie began his aviation training at the Wright Company in Dayton, Ohio. By this time, Curtiss had developed the A-1, A-2, and his newest plane, the hydroaeroplane or floatplane. After just two short months of training and learning how these planes worked, Eddie was given the opportunity to learn how to keep them in the air.

To do this, Eddie then headed off to the Naval Air Station at Pensacola, Florida. In March 1915, Ensign McDonnell was designated a Naval aviator, the eighteenth officer to be awarded this distinction. In addition, Edward was selected to be an aviation instructor at Pensacola and promoted to lieutenant junior grade in June 1915. These circumstances would alter and shape the course of my mother's family forever.

One of my favorite stories involving my grandfather was how he met my grandmother Helen Fisher. Shortly after accepting an instructor position at Pensacola, Eddie was heading to the local Catholic church. While leaving Sunday services, he spied two lovely young ladies who had just attended service at the much larger Presbyterian Church across the street.

According to the story, both services had just let out. Eddie had spied and followed these two young and quite attractive sisters toward Morrison's Cafeteria near downtown.

These young ladies turned out to be the Fisher sisters, Helen and Ralphine. Not only were they beautiful, but they came from one of the wealthiest families in this part of northern Florida. My mother, being a good Catholic herself, recalled that, while her father never fully converted, he did manage to attend the Presbyterian Church, in his dress white uniform, for several months afterward. From that point on, Eddie spent his off-duty hours courting Helen at her mother's—Sugar Pie Fisher's—enormous home on North Palafox Street.

Apparently, Helen was quite taken with this fine young men as well. My grandfather got engaged and was married on November 14, 1915.

Shortly after Eddie and Helen's wedding, his good friend and Annapolis classmate Charlie Mason arrived in Pensacola for aviation training. After being introduced to a second Fisher sister, Ralphine, Charlie too began the courting process. And that is how Charles P. Mason, the first commander of NAS Jacksonville, the commander and hero of the aircraft carrier USS *Hornet* during World War II, became my great-uncle Charlie and eventually the mayor of Pensacola.

Captain Charles P. Mason with wife Ralphine F. Mason and FDR
at NAS Jacksonville, 1940

Soon after his marriage, Eddie was involved in another naval aviation first. It was Eddie who designed and oversaw construction of the first airplane to be built at NAS Pensacola. This aircraft was designated the McDonnell-152.

The next two years were spent training young aviators at NAS Pensacola. About eighteen months prior to my mother Betty's birth, to prove that Navy pilots were superior to Marine pilots, Eddie performed two consecutive loops in an N-9 plane on February 14, 1917. He needed to do two loops because a day earlier a Marine Corps pilot had successfully completed the first single loop in the same plane.

In early April of 1917, then President Woodrow Wilson asked Congress to declare war on Germany and its allies. In one of the most stirring speeches ever given before the joint Houses, Wilson declared, "To such a task we dedicate our lives and our fortunes, everything that we are and everything that we have, with the pride of those who know that the day has come when America is privileged to spend her blood and her might for the principles that gave her birth and happiness and the peace which she has treasured. God helping her, she can do no other."

On April 6, Congress gave its nearly unanimous approval and declared war on Germany.

About a year prior to the war declaration, a group of students at Yale formed the Yale University Flying Club. Thanks to the support of men like H.P. Davison, Foster Rockwell, and Colonel Thompson, members of the club had access to several Curtiss seaplanes and trained at Huntington Bay, New York.

Colonel Thompson and Eddie McDonnell, First Yale Unit, 1917

When hostilities in Europe escalated and it seemed inevitable that the United States would enter the war, this group of young Yale men, led by "Trubee" Davison, Earl Gould, and Artemus Gates, left the cold weather of New York and moved their operations to Florida. They were encamped at Palm Beach when the declaration came in early April. Suddenly these young men of wealth and status found themselves on active duty with the Navy. Those who had completed their initial flight training were commissioned officers; the others came on board as enlisted men. Together they formed "The First Yale Unit." And who better to serve as their first commanding officer than young Navy Lieutenant Edward Orrick McDonnell.

CHAPTER FIVE

I had heard of the Yale Unit, or "Millionaire's Squadron," from my mother. She later credited this interaction between her father and the members of the unit when he became a successful investment banker. Her brother, my uncle Edward, went to Yale, but left shortly before graduation to volunteer in the US Army Air Corps during World War II. So, it was fascinating to me to learn just how large a role my grandfather had in the training and commanding of this group of outstanding young college students.

After gathering more information about these young men, I asked myself, *What was the motivation of these young men to join the Yale Unit?* After all, it meant leaving school, their friends, and the wealth and privilege that they had enjoyed all their lives. Why would young men like F. T. Davison, Artemus Gates, and Albert Sturtevant be driven to join a fledgling service and risk their very lives on a war that most Americans wanted to avoid? The answer was quite simple and one I had heard my entire life: "To whom much is given, much is expected."

These privileged elites knew that they couldn't ask others to defend our freedoms, our country, and their riches, unless they were willing to so as well. Not only were they willing to do so, but they were willing to go to war as naval aviators, in unproven planes and with an extremely limited amount of training.

Initially, the Yale Flying Club was a civilian air patrol club set up by several student-athletes with the goal of preparing a volunteer group for the eventuality of entering the First World War. Many of the young men paid for their own flight training on Long Island. They did this while attending classes at Yale full time. It wasn't until Woodrow Wilson declared war that this civilian air club was transformed into an active-duty naval squadron.

It was into this group that a young Lieutenant McDonnell was assigned. He had been a flight instructor at Naval Air Station Pensacola and at Huntington, New York, so he was very familiar with the aircraft used and the training of young inexperienced pilots. The "Loot," as he was called, turned out to be the perfect fit for this group of young men. Make no mistake, Eddie had spent four long years at Annapolis and another five on board combat ships learning the discipline and methods of the regular Navy. But his demeanor and attitudes allowed him to be readily accepted by the unit. His intelligence and adaptability were strengths that were much appreciated when he reported to the new training facility at Palm Beach, Florida.

Eddie "The Loot" with members of the First Yale Unit
in Palm Beach, April 1917

Upon Eddie's arrival in Palm Beach, he found that the unit was quartered in several recently built training center barracks. These structures lacked everything, including indoor plumbing. It was hot, humid, and buggy. Few working planes, fewer spare parts, and even fewer mechanics meant that these young men would have to learn every aspect of naval aviation. Dirty coveralls and greasy hands and faces were the accepted norms. Long hours of building and rebuilding planes, tedious lectures, and regular military drills were occasionally interrupted by short training flights. Several weeks after reporting, he sent a note to his superiors about these young aviators:

At times good-natured, indulging in a good deal of horse-paly, and with a natural rivalry among the various crews, every man carried on work of the most serious and arduous character. Changing motors, shifting the planes on the runways, washing, painting, etc., were done with the help of a handful of civilian mechanics and helpers which skeleton force was increased by a few petty officers sent on from Pensacola a few days after I arrived.

Yet none of the young pilots complained or griped. This made Eddie's task a much easier endeavor. Instead of a bunch of rich, spoiled, ne'er-do-wells, Eddie found his young charges eager to learn and willing to help no matter the job at hand. It seemed their only distraction from this rigorous schedule was the occasional dinner/dance with some of the young lovelies who wintered in the Palm Beaches.

Unfortunately, the Curtis flying boats were not only unreliable, but they were extremely difficult to fly. Wind, water currents, and waves made simple takeoffs and landings nearly impossible some days. Several members of the unit were injured, including its founder, F. Trubee Davison. Davison was involved in a low-level test flight when his plane went down, and he was pinned beneath it. Eddie witnessed the crash, landed nearby, and pulled Trubee from under the plane.

Unfortunately, his back injury was so severe that he was no longer able to train and was sent back to New York to heal and recover. He never flew as a Navy aviator with the First Yale Unit during World War I. But according to Betty, Trubee always credited Eddie with saving his life, and the two men remained friends for the remainder of their lives.

The men of Yale were extremely quick studies. Their training was completed in record time and with tremendous results. Upon completing flight training, many of the Yale Unit's members were sent overseas. Some flew combat missions. One of its members, Ensign Ingalls, was the Navy's first air combat ace. Others proved invaluable as scouts or spotters, alerting ground forces as to the movements of the enemy forces. Unfortunately, several members were killed or captured during their service in the First World War.

In late July 1917, then Lieutenant McDonnell was assigned as an instructor to Naval Air Station Huntington Bay, New York. It was there that my grandfather completed another first. On August 14, 1917, Eddie launched the first torpedo from an aircraft. Unfortunately, the torpedo struck the water at a bad angle and ricocheted back up into the air. This errant torpedo nearly stuck the plane that Eddie was piloting. After many more successful attempts, the Navy was satisfied that the torpedo tactics demonstrated by Eddie were sound and needed to be implemented. Unfortunately, these same tactics were utilized with deadly effectiveness by the Japanese when they attacked Pearl Harbor at the start of World War II.

NAS Huntington Bay was Eddie's first exposure to New York City and the Long Island area. It must have made quite an impression. Later in 1920, after being injured, Eddie resigned his commission and entered the active reserves. It was during this period that he moved his family to a home near Oyster Bay, New York. Eventually he would build a family compound overlooking Long Island Sound in the small village of Mill Neck. This would become the McDonnell family home for the next forty years.

Another of Betty's favorite tales occurred near the end of World War I. She used to refer to it as the time her father flew over the Alps.

She would always go and get the gold and silver cigarette case that was inscribed to Eddie by Italian Count Gianni Battista Caproni. The story would always start the same way.

After Huntington Bay, Eddie had a brief assignment in the Office of the Chief of Naval Operations in Washington, DC. After his Washington duties were complete, he reported to the commander of US Naval Forces Operating in European waters. His mission was to determine the feasibility of a naval aerial bombing group in general and specifically if nighttime bombing raids were feasible. The English bomber, the Handley Page 0/400, was in use by the Royal Air Force and considered an adequate daylight bomber. Unfortunately, the limited supply and the relatively short range of these aircraft meant that other alternatives were needed. The Department of the Navy, upon the advice of Lieutenant McDonnell, explored the use of a larger Italian aircraft designed for aerial bombardment by Count Battista Caproni who had built a reputation on unique designs, cutting edge technology. He had also demonstrated the feasibility of aerial night bombings on a military industrial complex in Austria.

Unfortunately, some of this technology, including the 600-hp Fiat engine, had been used prematurely. Many of Caproni's aircraft were extremely unreliable and had a nasty problem with parts falling off while in flight.

Nevertheless, Eddie and several other members of the Yale Unit were sent to Milan to pick up six of Caproni's latest bomber, the C3. They were to fly the planes to Paullac NAS, France, and on to London. It just so happens that the Northern Bombing Group based at the naval air station there was commanded by Eddie's brother-in-law, Lieutenant Charles P. Mason.

The first bomber arrived on August 11, 1918. Its Fiat engine had to be rebuilt, and so the plane's first mission, a nighttime bombing raid on the German sub and shipping ports in Belgium, was not carried out until August 14. It was during this mission that Eddie further enhanced his reputation as fearless flier. He was attempting to drop a bomb on one of the U-boat pens when the armed bomb got stuck in the rack. So, after his typical calm assessment, Eddie simply stood in the cockpit, draped his leg over the side, and kicked the bomb loose. Problem solved.

He continued his service with the US Northern Bombing Group for several more months. In 1918, Eddie saw continued action and active air combat in Italy and France. He also engaged in the bombing of German submarine bases at Bruges, Zeebrugge, and Ostend. For his service in Europe during the First World War, Eddie was awarded the Navy Cross that read, *"For distinguished and heroic service as a pilot attached to U.S. Naval Aviation Forces Abroad. Took an important and valuable part in organizing U.S. Northern Bombing Group. Made several extremely hazardous flights over the Alps, in machines which were known to be structurally imperfect."*

Soon after these bombing raids, the First World War came to an end. Eddie was temporarily assigned brief duty at US Naval Headquarters in London in connection with the delivery of aircraft for the battleship USS *Texas*. The British built Sopwith Camel 2F.1 was chosen for this rather dangerous task onboard the American battleship.

In September of 1918, Eddie was promoted to lieutenant commander and assigned to the battleship *Texas*, an older style battleship whose keel was laid in early 1911. It served in both World Wars and is now a museum outside of Houston.

At first, I thought that the reason for my grandfather's assignment to the *Texas* was simply to transport him back to the US after the war. I later discovered that the true purpose of this assignment was to allow Eddie time to develop, design, and supervise the building of an experimental ramp in order to test his theory about scout planes and the viability of placing them onto the decks of the large ships of the line, such as battleships and cruisers.

He spent his time on board studying the ships layout and determining the best place to build the launch platform. It was decided that the top of turrets two and three offered the most space and gave the plane just enough runway to "hopefully" get airborne. Early in January of 1919, Eddie was assigned to the Office of Naval Operations, as well as the Naval Bureau of Navigation. He was given command of the first (USS *Texas*) and eventually the second (USS *Mississippi*) US Navy ship plane units. When he arrived at Guantanamo Bay, Cuba, it was decided that Eddie would first launch from the *Texas* and then continue upon an exploratory flight throughout Central and South America.

USS Texas with aircraft installed, Guantanamo Bay, Cuba, March 1919.

On March 9, 1919, a surplus World War I plane, a Sopwith 2F.1 Camel from the Conde Bluff Camp at Guantanamo Bay, was brought aboard the *Texas* and placed upon the platform atop gun turret two. The following day, March 10, at approximately 4:45 p.m., Lt. Commander Edward O. McDonnell (Naval Aviator No. 18) climbed into the cockpit of the airplane and successfully took off from the *Texas*. It was remarkable not only because it was the first flight off a US battleship but also because the launch platform was only forty-four feet from the wheels of the plane to the end of the ramp. They had to use a slingshot approach to launch the plane. Even though the plane was at full power when they removed the wheel chocks, the small aircraft still seemed to fall off the end of the platform. It nearly hit the water before it regained altitude and became fully airborne.

Eddie preparing for takeoff from the USS *Texas*, 1919.

After launching from the *Texas*, Eddie continued on a remarkable flight throughout the Caribbean Sea. He visited islands and countries in South and Central America. He flew across uncharted waters navigating by sight and a simple compass.

My mother later admitted that her father had told her that the launch and flights were truly terrifying, but they were experiences that later would prove invaluable in his career as an aviation expert in the investment banking industry.

A short time after his historic flight from the battleship, Eddie was attempting to break the flight-time record from New York to Washington in a new Navy aircraft. As he approached Hog Island on the Delaware River, his engine cut out, and he began to lose altitude. According to several witnesses, the plane plunged from the sky in a steep dive and crash-landed into a nearby swamp.

When the rescuers arrived, they found Eddie buried in thick black mud. He was not breathing, and they detected no pulse. The ambulance then rushed him to a nearby hospital. When he arrived, Eddie was still not breathing, and the doctors could not get a pulse. They covered him with a sheet and declared him dead. They even went so far as to call and inform his mother and wife that Eddie had passed away.

About an hour later, after the staff had cleaned the mud and muck from his body, they set it on a stretcher for transport to the local mortuary. While loading the body, the sheet covering his face had slipped off. One of the staff was about to replace the sheet when they noticed one of his eyelids twitching. They quickly called a nurse and doctor who, upon seeing Eddie, immediately called back his grieving mother and wife. Poor medical equipment and improper training had led the staff to believe he was dead.

Eddie had proven once again that he was one extremely lucky and tough naval aviator. Unfortunately, this accident caused a serious back injury that would force him to leave active duty a short time later and plague him for the rest of his life.

Soon after Eddie had recovered from this mishap, he was once again part of a serious and dangerous aviation experience. This one involved his good friend, classmate, and brother-in-law Charlie P. Mason.

My great-uncle Charlie had been given command of a newly formed Naval special squadron designated VS Squadron 3 at NAS Anacostia, just outside Washington, DC. Charlie oversaw developing a long-range scouting plane for the Navy, and had invited Eddie along for a test flight. As fate would have it, everything went smoothly until the plane landed.

Eddie was at the controls. While the flaps were functioning, the braking mechanism on the plane had failed. So, these two pilots did the only thing they could think of. While Eddie continued to steer the plane down the runway, Charlie opened the cockpit door and dragged his booted foot along the tarmac until the plane finally came to a stop. It was quite the sight, and word spread quickly of the adventure these two senior officers had experienced. These two were taunted, then toasted, when they arrived at the base officers' club later that day.

CHAPTER SIX

After his assignment aboard the USS *Texas* was complete, Eddie had reported for duty at the Bureau of Navigation and the Office of Naval Operations, the Navy Department in Washington, DC. It was during this period that the plane crash had damaged his spine beyond repair. So, effective January 11, 1920, Eddie resigned from active duty. About a month later, he accepted an appointment as a lieutenant commander in the US Naval Reserve Force (Aviation).

He joined the active reserves to stay up to date on the latest military aircraft and the technologies that went along with them. Eddie spent months in active training duty at NAS Rockaway Beach, Long Island, and at NAS Pensacola. He also had active-duty assignments on board the USS *Wright*, which at the time was the Flagship of Commander Aircraft Squadrons, Scouting Fleet.

This was truly the Golden Age of both military and civilian aircraft. New applications, including mail and passenger services, were transformed by these new, faster delivery transportation methods.

New York banks and investment houses where scrambling to gain the upper hand on their competition. Aviation experts were in short supply and high demand.

None more so than Edward O. McDonnell. His early flight experiences and active-duty training sessions kept him at the forefront of this new technology. When he served on board the USS *Wright* (AV-

1), in 1923, Eddie learned firsthand about "lighter-than-air" aircraft. When the *Wright* was later rebuilt as a seaplane tender, Eddie was there to learn about this important aviation application and how it could be adapted to civilian and commercial use.

It was during this period of active duty aboard the *Wright* that Eddie served under Captain Ernest J. King. These two men would remain great friends for the rest of their lives. This was the same Ernest King who would later be promoted to fleet admiral and CNO during World War II. He was on the Joint Chiefs of Staff and made sure that his good friend Eddie was in command of an escort carrier group during certain critical battles at the close of the Second World War.

During his time in the active reserves while serving at these different naval air stations, Eddie was able to improve his flying skills using the latest military aircraft. He was also able to identify and train the best and the brightest young naval aviators. Many of these young men would later be recruited for civilian jobs with the aviation companies that Eddie helped create and finance while working on Wall Street. All these duties enabled Eddie to remain at the pinnacle of the aviation industry, apprised of any new military developments and applications. Eddie was soon recognized as the leading aviation expert of his time.

Shortly after joining the active Naval Reserves, Eddie was contacted by one of the young men he commanded during his time with the First Yale Aviation Unit. One of this flyer's family members had a connection with the investment banking firm of Grayson M.P. Murphy.

Grayson Murphy was a West Point graduate who served during World War I and was instrumental in funding and capitalizing growing companies in the transportation industries. Murphy was convinced that aviation was going to become a huge part of those industries. Grayson Murphy accepted the recommendation and hired the Loot. He knew that Eddie's knowledge and experience in the fledgling aviation field would be an invaluable asset to the firm. Murphy never regretted this decision.

Eddie on Wall Street with Grayson
M.P. Murphy, 1923.

After learning the investment banking industry for several years and having worked his way up to a junior partner, Eddie was a critical component when Juan Terry Trippe approached Grayson M.P. Murphy with an idea about commercial airlines in 1927. Trippe, a Yale graduate and Naval aviator during World War I, knew Eddie and wanted him on his team. He had personally selected the investment firm of Grayson M.P. Murphy because of his relationship with Eddie McDonnell.

Trippe, whose backers included Cornelius Vanderbilt Whitney, W. Averell Harriman, and Henry "Hap" Arnold, wanted Grayson Murphy to handle the selling of stock shares to finance his start-up company, Pan American Airlines (The Aviation Corporation of the Americas).

Trippe had acquired the landing and mail service rights to Havana, a modern, cosmopolitan city, which at the time was considered the hub of the Caribbean and Central American area.

Trippe's airline vision did not extend into the areas of aircraft design, route navigation, and suitability standards that our government had placed upon this new industry. Grayson M.P. Murphy had insisted that one of its own be placed on the board of directors of Pan Am. They selected Eddie McDonnell.

In September of 1929, Trippe and Charles Lindbergh began touring Central and South America to negotiate landing rights and acquire aircraft for their operations. Eddie, who had been one of the first pilots to have flown the region back in 1919, joined them.

This was also the year that shipping and chemical giant W.R. Grace & Company formed a fifty-fifty joint venture with Pan Am to facilitate both companies' entry into the Central and South American markets. This was important because they needed to speed up the transportation of key materials and personnel, as well as to improve the communications between its operations. An interesting side note to this joint venture was that my mother's sister Ann would later marry into the Grace family. She and her husband Oliver Grace would have three beautiful daughters, my cousins, Helen, "Little Ann," and Ruth.

Over the coming years, other companies followed suit. Eddie's successes with Pan American made him a very hot commodity in the aviation and transportation industries. Companies such as Boeing, United Aircraft, Hertz Car Rental, and the Pacific Zeppelin Transport Company all wanted this brash but brilliant young aviator on their Board of Directors. Eddie was happy to oblige and instrumental in providing much of the early capital that these companies required to grow.

In 1934, Trippe knew it was time to connect the west coast of America to the Far East. Asia's vast resources and large population centers were going to play a critical role in the growth of both civilian and military aviation in the coming years. My grandfather had already taken part in the initial survey of the south Pacific and Asia as both a member of Pan American's board and as a naval observer, so his insight proved invaluable.

Eddie, with his Navy connections, would also be a tremendous asset in securing the necessary permission to utilize military airstrips, ports, and refueling stations that an aircraft and airline would require in order to operate over these enormous stretches of ocean. Pan Am negotiated the landing rights at Pearl Harbor, Midway, Wake Island, Guam, and Subic Bay, Philippines. This was necessary due to the slower speeds and frequent refueling that these early passenger planes required to cross the vast Pacific Ocean.

In March of 1935, Pan American leased the merchant vessel *North Haven* and shipped out over $500,000 worth of aviation and aircraft materials to all its landing zones and refueling stations. One month later, Trippe sent out a survey crew to finalize its operations at each of its ports of call. Pan Am was awarded the mail contract between San Francisco and Canton, China.

On November 22, 1935, the first mail service flight took off from Alameda County, California. It arrived in Manilla seven days later and returned to San Francisco Bay on December 6. It had completed the almost 16,000-mile roundtrip in just fourteen days. This roundtrip service had cut the time of the fastest steamship by over two weeks. Of course, Eddie had been allowed to participate in this inaugural flight. Eleven months later, in October 1936, the first commercial passenger flight took off from San Francisco and landed in Manilla six days later. Passengers included Edward McDonnell and his wife, Helen. The cost was a staggering $1,750 roundtrip, or about $17,000 in today's dollars.

After conquering the Pacific and developing routes into the Asian markets, Pan American set its sights on Europe. Almost all the travel to Europe took place aboard steamships and ocean liners. But these ships took many days, or often weeks, to cross the Atlantic Ocean. Businessman and seasoned, well-healed travelers wanted a faster alternative to these floating hotels. This would mark the start of the golden age of commercial, gas-filled airships (or zeppelins).

It was because of Eddie's role on the board of Pan American that he was invited by Juan Trippe to join the board of the Pacific Zeppelin Transport Company. His board membership and aviation knowledge were the reasons that he was included on one of the most remarkable flights in history. It was called the Millionaires Flight, and after some research, I realized that it occurred aboard the German airship Hindenburg.

Unfortunately, I didn't realize this while listening to and learning about one of the more unusual stories from my mother. Most of the important details were left out. But one thing stands clear. The truly important details, at least in her mind, were the train's luxurious accommodations and the extraordinary meals served on board. Not mentioned were the reasons for the flight, or the remarkable list of passengers on board the Hindenburg. Here is a partial list:

Karl Lindemann
Director of the Hamburg-Amerika Line and an officer of Standard Oil

Paul W. Litchfield
President of Goodyear Tire & Rubber, and the leading force behind American commercial airship endeavors

Hans Luther
German ambassador to the United States; Former chancellor and President of Germany and President of the Reichsbank

Paul MacKall
Bethlehem Steel Executive

Lucius B. Manning
President, Cord Automobile Corporation

Thomas McCarter
Former New Jersey Attorney General and founder of the Public Service Corporation of New Jersey, one of America's largest utility companies

Edward O. McDonnell
Director of Pan American Airways; Banker with Grayson M.P. Murphy (an investor in the Pacific Zeppelin Transport Co., of which McDonnell was a director)

Joachim Meyer

R. Walton Moore
U.S. Assistant Secretary of State

Juan and Betty Trippe disembarking Hindenburg after a flight from Frankfurt to Rio de Janeiro, 1936 (photo Elizabeth Trippe, courtesy panam.org)

The story of the Millionaires Flight was truly a perfect example of how business was conducted back in the 1930s. The flight was organized by the Deutsche Zeppelin-Reederei (DZR) and Standard Oil of New Jersey (Esso) to stimulate interest and investors in a joint American-German passenger service using the DZR's airships. Many experts thought that the future of air travel to and from the European continent would include these fast, luxurious zeppelins.

The passenger list read like a who's who of American industry, finance, aviation, and government. Names like Nelson Rockefeller, Winthrop W. Aldrich, Eddie Rickenbacker, Jack Frye, and Juan Trippe all took part on this historic flight. My grandfather's role was to assess the viability and functionality of these aircraft when compared with the more traditional fix-wing planes that Pan American had utilized in conquering the Pacific. As an investment banker, Eddie was also instrumental in looking into the financial aspects of merging with a pre-World War II German company. This would certainly have required additional investigation and due diligence.

The Pacific Zeppelin Transport Company had been founded in 1929 to operate airship service between California and Hawaii. Until then, if you wanted to go to Hawaii or needed to transport materials, you used a ship. Obviously, this method of transportation could often take weeks to arrive in these extremely remote islands.

Juan Trippe had been an early investor in PZT Co. He knew that people would pay for the speed and comfort that the zeppelins could provide. But both he and Eddie McDonnell had seen the advantages that fixed-wing aircraft, like the Pan Am Clippers, brought to the fledgling airline industry. Much faster service meant much larger revenues. It was likely that many of the passengers, like Trippe, Frye, Rickenbacker, and my grandfather were simply there to confirm their suspicions. They were there to check up on the possible competition should they decide not to merge their operations.

Nevertheless, the festivities began around midnight on October 8, 1936, at New York's Penn Station. A late-night snack and copious amounts of fine alcoholic beverages were available to the guests just prior to them retiring to their luxurious sleeping accommodations. The trip featured specially chartered Pullman cars that this group of giants from the political, military, and industrial complex would travel in through the night to Lakehurst, New Jersey. Promptly at 5:00 a.m., the passengers were awakened and treated to a gourmet breakfast before boarding the Hindenburg for the 6:57 a.m. flight.

The flight path of the giant airship was up the Hudson River Valley, then east over New England to view the beautiful fall foliage in eastern Massachusetts.

Lunch was to be served while circling Boston. It was a copy of the lunch menu that my mother still had that led us into this conversation in the first place. The menu included Indian swallow nest soup followed by cold Rhine salmon and Carmen salad. The main course included tenderloin steak with goose liver sauce, chateau potatoes, beans *a la Princesses,* and iced melon. Of course, there was plenty of wine and good German ale to wash it all down. All this was followed by Turkish coffee, pastries, and fine liqueurs. It was safe to say that no expense was sparred to impress its guests.

After lunch, the airship turned south heading back toward New York City and its final destination at Lakehurst, New Jersey. It is of interest that the American Airlines DC-3 that was scheduled to return the passengers to New York City was grounded due to heavy fog in New Jersey. One of the few advantages the zeppelins had over planes was their ability to navigate in bad weather due to the slower speeds and altitude requirements.

The Hindenburg landed without incident and shortly thereafter took off for its final Atlantic crossing of the 1936 season. Unfortunately, the following year, on its first flight back across the Atlantic, the Hindenburg met its fiery end while docking at its mooring post in Lakehurst. This signaled the end of the gracious age of travel on these giant gas-filled zeppelins.

After determining that the future of civilian aircraft and commercial travel was going to be better served by fixed-wing aircraft, Juan Trippe and his airline set its sights on flying to Europe.

In the summer of 1937, Pan American again sent survey crews out to inspect routes from Port Washington, New York, to both England and France. Upon their return, it was decided that a preferable, more central location from which to depart was on the Mid-Atlantic coast. The route they selected left from Norfolk, Virginia, flew to Bermuda, and on to Europe via the Azores. The limited fuel capacity and high fuel usage of these aircraft required frequent stops.

Several years later, in 1939, the first commercial air service began from Port Washington on the north shore of Long Island. Of course, Eddie and Helen McDonnell, as well as most of the Pan Am's board of directors, were on Pan American's Dixie Clipper, the first commercial passenger flight across the Atlantic Ocean to Europe.

Eddie (far right) and Helen (seated second from right)
waiting to board Pan American's *Dixie Clipper*

One of the more humorous tales to emerge from the flight was the story my mother loved to tell. After landing outside Paris, the board of Pan Am left on a luxury train coach for Rome and a private audience with the Pope. As usual, the story was embellished by my mother who described the food served along the train's route. Betty insisted that her father much preferred the French chef who prepared the meals on the way to Rome. Eddie felt that he was far superior to the Italian chef who served the passengers on the return trip.

My grandmother Helen would usually correct my mother by explaining that after a while, all that rich food, whether French or Italian, became almost tedious and mundane. Betty would then interrupt her and calmly point out that she never heard her father complain about the richness of the food. She would then gently goad her mother by saying that her father Eddie obviously had a much more sophisticate palate when it came to gourmet dining.

Several days after Pan American's board arrived in Rome, they had their scheduled meeting at the Vatican. After being escorted into the Pope's audience chamber, the board members were kept waiting for almost an hour. The only chair in this room was the "Pope's Throne." My grandmother Helen, a notorious complainer, got fed up with waiting.

She decided to sit on the only chair available, the Throne. She managed to ignore all the other attendee's calls to remove herself until one of the cardinals came into the room. He was aghast, and demanded that Helen get up immediately. She responded by saying that she was tired of waiting and it was perfectly acceptable for her to sit on the only available chair in the chamber.

"You see," she told the stunned cardinal in front of her embarrassed husband, "it's alright for me to sit down because I'm a Presbyterian, and the Catholic rules don't apply." The entire board erupted in laughter, and even the cardinal had to chuckle.

Another quick story that always brought a twinkle to my mother's eyes was set at the River Club in New York. I could not verify this through the club, but several family members did confirm this story.

While still an investment banker and newly a senior partner with Grayson M.P. Murphy, a very powerful political figure from Boston wanted to join this very exclusive club on the East River. Well, several of the senior members strongly objected to allowing that "Bootlegging Boston" wannabe to join their club.

Knowing Eddie's temperament and his no nonsense manner, they approached him and asked how they should handle this rather delicate situation. His response was simple—call a member vote and let the chips fall where they may. Well, long story short, Mr. Joseph Kennedy was kept from joining New York's River Club because of several "black balls" in the voting vessel. My mother was still in possession of her father's black marble years later. She, like her father Eddie, never did get along well with Democrats.

In October of 1937, Grayson Murphy passed away. Soon afterward, the firm bearing his name merged with Hornblower and

Weeks. Hornblower, based in Boston, was an established investment banking firm that was interested in exploring the profit potential of the aviation and travel industries. By merging with Grayson Murphy, they not only increased the market value of the firm, but they also gained valuable entrance into these growing industries.

One of the stipulations of the merger was that Hornblower was to gain the seats on the boards that Grayson Murphy controlled. These seats included membership on the boards of Pan Am, Boeing, and the Lockheed group. One other critical aspect of the merger was getting Eddie McDonnell to agree to join the executive staff of Hornblower. Eddie's knowledge and expertise were nearly as important as gaining control of the seats on the boards that the Murphy teams had occupied. He was brought on board as a senior partner and given control of the aviation and aeronautics division within Hornblower. This was how Eddie continued building on his legacy as an aviation expert, generated huge salaries, and earned exorbitant bonuses.

In 1938, still at the height of the Great Depression, Eddie's salary was over $100,000 annually, and according to Betty, her father received a year-end bonus of over $250,000. In today's dollars, that would be equivalent to about a $2.5 million and a $7 million bonus. In July 1940, Eddie, who, at the time, was still in the active Navy reserves, was promoted to commander and assigned as a naval observer on Pan American's first extended flight to New Zealand, Australia, and the islands of the Dutch East Indies. This was understandable since he would have been on the Pan Am flights whether as an observer or board member.

But there was something deeper going on. At first, I didn't understand the connection between his promotion and this first exploratory flight of a commercial airlines. But upon further examination, this connection became quite clear. The US military in general, and the Navy in particular, were very interested in this region of the world. The Empire of Japan needed certain raw materials to maintain their growing armed forces and military industries. Securing these vital resources and maintaining a quiet military presence were priorities for the Japanese.

Many of the locations that Pan American Airlines were interested in were also regions that Japan coveted and needed. The flights to New Zealand, Australia, and the Dutch East Indies took several months to complete. After completing his assessment for Pan American's board, and making his recommendations to the investment board at Hornblower & Weeks, Eddie returned to active duty with the Navy. And to no one's surprise, his first assignment was at the Naval Bureau of Aeronautics in Washington DC.

After several months in Washington, Eddie was assigned as the attaché for air in London. England had always maintained a large military-industrial presence in the southern Pacific and Asia. Great Britain and her allies needed the latest, most updated information. What Eddie provided would play a major role in the defense of Australia and New Zealand.

After several months in London, Eddie was transferred to Beijing, known as Peiping at the time. There, he worked with the Chinese and their allies in the same capacity as the US attaché for air. They too were interested in the information that only Eddie could provide. In addition, Eddie proved invaluable in assessing the Chinese air force and other military resources. He provided the necessary intelligence for the Chinese to defend their resource-rich areas from the Japanese aggressors.

He was also included as a member of the first US air mission to China. For his vital contributions to this cause, Eddie was awarded the Air Medal, with the inscription:

> *For meritorious achievement in aerial flight as a Member of the First Air Mission to China, May and June of 1941. As naval member (of that mission), Commander McDonnell participated in numerous hazardous flights in Chinese Air Force planes over enemy Japanese held territory despite intense*

opposition from hostile forces and thereby gained information of great value in establishing a better understanding between the military air forces of China and the United States. His outstanding professional knowledge, unwavering devotion to duty and gallant conduct throughout this vital mission reflect the highest credit upon Captain (then Commander) McDonnell and the United States Naval Service.

CHAPTER SEVEN

While World War II was raging in the European theater, America was still hoping to avoid entry into the war. Helping England with spare ships and aircraft was one thing. Risking American lives so soon after the First World War was quite another. Appeasers like British Prime Minister Neville Chamberlain and American Ambassador Joseph Kennedy had convinced many Americans that Hitler and his allies, Italy and Japan, posed little or no threat to our country.

Eddie knew a different side. While serving as the attaché for air in London in early 1941, Eddie had lived through much of the Battle of Britain. He had seen firsthand what the German Luftwaffe was capable of. Their aircraft were superior in nearly every respect to planes flown by the RAF, our Navy, and Army Air Corps. Germany's pilots had gained valuable experience during the Spanish Civil War and during the early days of World War II. They too were superior to all but the most senior of the British and volunteer American pilots who flew against them. If not for the skill of a few British pilots and the Rolls Royce Merlin engines that powered their Spitfires and Hurricanes, Britain and the war in Europe would have been lost.

Eddie also saw the absolute necessity in pilot training. No matter how good an aircraft, an inexperienced and poorly trained pilot stood no chance against battle-hardened veterans. He knew that superior aircraft technology and weaponry were also necessary to compete with the Axis forces. This became abundantly clear to him while watching the slaughter in the skies above England.

Eddie's experience further cemented these beliefs. Like the Germans, the Japanese had a tremendous advantage in both aircraft technology and in the number of experienced pilots at their command. He had witnessed Japan's buildup, aggression, and complete disregard for human life during the Chinese campaigns just prior to the start of World War II.

As stated before, Eddie, during his earlier trips to Asia, had come to realize that Japan was looking for resources to supplement and help grow its military and industrial might. Steel, oil, and rubber were vital for Japan to become a world power.

Part of Eddie's mission to the southeastern Pacific with Pan Am was to scout islands for naval and air bases. This was done under the guise of searching for profitable markets and commercial landing locations for Pan Am. He was also there to make assessments on the growing Japanese threats in the region and make recommendations for the defense of critical reserves and our ally's strategic military operations.

Upon his return from Great Britain and China in July 1941, Eddie was given command of the Naval Air Station at New York City. This station was primarily responsible for the defense of the northeastern Atlantic coast, as well as training new Navy pilots and developing new aviation technologies.

In addition, Eddie also served as the district aviation officer for the Third Naval District. One interesting side note was that even though Eddie's brother John McDonnell was not an aviator, he was given command of Mitchel Field on Long Island. As Betty loved pointing out, the main air defense for the entire northeastern coast of the United States was in the extremely capable hands of the McDonnell brothers.

Because of his experiences in England and China, Eddie realized early on that the United States would have little or no option when it came to entering World War II. So, on November 20, 1941, just prior to the attack on Pearl Harbor, Eddie's only son, Edward Jr. joined the Army Air Corps. Shortly after Edward Jr.'s enlistment in December 1941, Eddie McDonnell was promoted to captain.

Like so many before him, another child of wealth and privilege had recognized his duty prior to being called. The First Yale Unit had been volunteers. So too was Theodore Roosevelt and so many others. They didn't need to serve, but they certainly felt as though they needed to give back to a country that had given them so much. Later in World War II, George H. W. Bush and Eddie McDonnell each requested combat assignments and risked their very lives for this great nation. Once again, to whom much is given, from them much is owed.

Edward Jr. had about a year and a half left before graduating from Yale in the class of '43. He enlisted as an aviation cadet. After advanced fighter training at Grenier Field in Manchester, New Hampshire, he received his commission as a second lieutenant on August 5, 1942. This was less than nine months after his enlistment.

Second Lieutenant Edward O. McDonnell Jr. 1942.

Another of Betty's favorite stories happened shortly after Edward Jr.'s commissioning. Young Edward had graduated in 1939 from St. Paul's School, which was a few miles from the Grenier, New Hampshire, Air Base. The boys at the school had gotten so used to the aircraft noises that they could tell what type of plane was flying overhead just by the sound of its engines.

One day, a very loud Curtis P-40 engine was flying quite low over the school. It buzzed the roofs of Old Upper and Hargate Halls. After skimming the library and Simpson Hall, the plane made a final pass over the playing fields.

To the pilot's amazement, all of students assembled in a *V* formation and were saluting the plane. In return, the pilot performed a barrel roll at very high speed just yards off the ground. The students learned that the pilot was Second Lieutenant Edward O. McDonnell Jr. when he visited St. Paul's just a few days later to thank them and to say goodbye.

After the visit to his old school, "Boy," as he was called by his family, left for his first posting in North Africa. Edward Jr. was assigned to the 87th Fighter Squadron, which was part of the 79th Fighter Group. The 87th Fighter Squadron was a newly formed P-40 squadron assigned to the British Eighth Army based in Tunisia. Their duties included ground support for the infantry and tank commands, as well as flying cover for the bombers that were striking at enemy positions throughout the region.

According to my mother, her father was very upset that his son had chosen the Army Air Corps. He knew the quality of the planes the Army flew and realized that his son would be flying in a considerably inferior aircraft.

Edward O. McDonnell Jr. (Boy) Army Air Forces diploma, 1942.

The Curtis P-40 was well known as the plane of the "Flying Tigers" in China. When Eddie had served in Beijing, he became quite familiar with the limitations of this aircraft. Truth be told, the P-40 was underpowered, heavy, and thought of as un-maneuverable and almost clumsy. Matched against the Messerschmitt ME-109, the Curtis P-40 proved to be a huge disappointment and placed the allied pilots at a tremendous disadvantage when engaged with the far superior German aircraft.

Lieutenant Edward O. McDonnell Jr. in front of his Curtis P-40, 1942.

On April 2, 1943, while on his ninth sortie, Edward Jr. took off on a routine bomber support mission in the fighter he named the *Barbara Ann*. His mission involved flying over the Mediterranean Sea so that a squadron of bombers could attack German and Italian coastal installations.

Because of the poor performance of the P-40, Edward Jr's squadron had lost several of its most senior pilots. Their replacements were eager, but they were also raw and inexperienced. While flying toward their intended target, a group of ME-109s was spotted in the distance. Instead of continuing on to the target and escorting the bomber group, Edward Jr's new and inexperienced wingman didn't follow procedures and went after what he thought was a single enemy plane.

Ignoring Edward's warning, he soon realized that he had been baited by the German pilots and was now being chased by at least three Messerschmitts. While the bombers continued toward their target, Edward Jr. went after his wingman. According to reports, Edward Jr. downed one plane and was targeting another when he was hit and began spiraling toward the sea. He managed to bail out and landed about a half-mile off the beach. Unfortunately, his chute did not spill its air, and another pilot reported seeing young Edward being dragged across the water. The pilot dove and flattened the parachute with the backwash of his plane's propeller. He then reported that Edward Jr. appeared to be severely injured and that the Germans had sent a boat out to pick him up. The final sighting of Lieutenant Edward O. McDonnell was of him floating face down in the Mediterranean Sea as a German gunboat approached. He was buried by the Germans, and years later, his ashes were reinterred at Arlington National Cemetery in the same grave as his father. Edward Orrick McDonnell had lost his only son and namesake.

Edward O. McDonnell Jr.'s Gold Star Citation

My mother Betty always had great difficulty discussing the death of her younger brother, Boy. She was extremely close to him and realized that the entire dynamics of her immediate family had profoundly changed after his death.

My grandmother Helen became very depressed and began to imbibe heavily. Her moodiness and sullen attitudes were very troubling to all those who knew her. She became withdrawn and isolated. Seemingly, the only two people she would communicate with were Eddie and her granddaughter Kathleen, my mother's daughter from her first marriage. Unfortunately, most of the communication with Eddie was criticism. She blamed him for not insisting on Navy service and not protecting her son better.

Kathleen had been born while Betty's first husband was stationed in the Philippines. My mother had returned to the United States when the threat of a war with Japan seemed imminent. Eddie had warned her and insisted that she and her young child come back to the New York area. Betty and Kathleen had been splitting time between her family's home in Mill Neck, Long Island, and an apartment in New York City that she shared with her sister Ann.

It was during this time that my grandmother developed a tremendous affection for her young granddaughter. Kathleen was spending more and more time at her grandparent's home. After the death of her son Edward Jr., Helen transferred most of what was left of her motherly instincts toward Kathleen. Betty would comment in later years that Kathleen had replaced her and her sister Ann as the favorite member of the family.

Immediately following the death of Edward Jr., Helen would sit for hours, smoking and often weeping quietly, while thinking of her lost son. Helen also began to drink excessively. She had always been a social drinker, but she was now turning into a raging alcoholic.

Eddie had also changed after the loss of his son. He had always been a hard worker, but he became almost obsessed. He spent long hours away from home and traveling to different posts, performing inspections and improving the training methods of the young aviators under his care. Sensing that both he and his wife needed a change of scenery, Eddie requested and received a transfer from the New York area.

In June of 1943, Eddie reported as chief of staff and aide to the commandant, Naval Air Training Center, Corpus Christi, Texas. About nine months later, he was transferred and named the chief of staff of Naval Air Intermediate Training Command.

Eddie knew that he could never bring back his son. But he also realized that he might be able to save other families from the same tragedy and sorrow by training these young Navy aviators to be the best pilots in the world. Shortly thereafter, much to Helen's utter dismay, Eddie quested a combat command.

I often wondered why a fifty-three-year-old multimillionaire would risk everything, including his life, and request a combat command. Again, Betty provided me with an answer.

Her father had requested a combat command because he felt it was his duty. After training so many young men to fly, and then seeing them put in harm's way, Eddie knew it was his turn to do his part. He had been trained for combat. He was a warrior, and he knew that the front lines was where he could do the most good.

Rarely, if ever, were senior active Naval Reserve officers given ships or battle commands. But Eddie had an advantage. He approached one of his old commanders and requested a combat assignment. Fleet Admiral and Naval Chief of Staff Ernest King agreed to allow Eddie to command a carrier group. Eddie had known that the chances of him receiving a combat command were slim at best. But in May of 1944, Eddie was detached to the headquarters of Twelfth Naval District in San Francisco. There, he was given command of the USS *Long Island* (CVE-1).

The *Long Island* was a converted cargo liner that, when refitted and recommissioned, became the first escort carrier in the US Navy. Upon completion, this first "baby flattop" was stationed out of Norfolk, Virginia, and was considered an experimental ship. The Navy wanted to test the feasibility of using converted cargo ships as small, fast carriers both in battle and for training new naval aviators.

The *Long Island*, after months of testing, showed real promise and value. She was then outfitted with a full complement of aircraft and sent to the Pacific theater. In August of 1942, she got her first taste of action, providing air cover and supporting Marines at the Battle of Guadalcanal. She performed splendidly.

Next, she was sent back to San Diego to train Navy aviators. The early years of the war had taken their toll on experienced pilots, and the *Long Island* needed replacements. After about eighteen months in San Diego, the ship was ordered back into combat. It was at this point that Eddie took command.

The *Long Island*'s first mission was to transport a variety of needed materials to various outposts in the Pacific theater, which included aircraft, replacement parts, and air crews. These were sent to resupply the larger frontline carriers and airfields.

Eddie in command of and on deck of the USS *Long Island*, 1944.

It was toward the end of his command that Eddie faced his biggest challenge aboard the *Long Island*. In mid-December 1944, a huge tropical storm called Typhoon Cobra struck the main body of the Pacific fleet. Winds exceeding 150 mph and waves exceeding sixty feet were recorded. According to Betty, her father convinced several of his superiors, including Admiral William "Bull" Halsey, to suspend fueling operations and head northwest out of the typhoons path.

As the weather improved, Halsey, for some unknown reason, decided to again change course and head due south. Unfortunately, this led the 3rd Fleet straight into the eye of the storm. In the end, three destroyers were lost, and numerous other ships were heavily damaged.

In addition to the ships, nearly 790 sailors and Marines lost their lives because of faulty weather information and the inability to accurately locate and track this monster storm.

Shortly after Typhoon Cobra ended, Eddie was given command of the USS *Nehenta Bay* (CVE-74). Commissioned in January 1944, the *Nehenta Bay* was one of the newest escort carriers in the Navy's fleet. During her short operational history, she had built an impressive battle record. The escort carrier had provided critical air support in the Mariana and Palau Island campaigns. She had also been involved in the battles of Tinian and Saipan. The *Nehenta Bay* had been one of the ships damaged during the typhoon. A monster wave, estimated at over seventy feet, had struck the carrier on her flight deck and collapsed several deck supports near her bow. The ship stayed in the southern Pacific waters while repairs were made. It was truly remarkable that these extensive repairs took a little over a week to complete.

When Eddie took command on December 27, 1944, the escort carrier was part of a large carrier task force that was finally heading back to the South China Sea area after a three-year absence. Days of fierce battles ensued, and Eddie was again rewarded for his heroic deeds. This time he received the Bronze Star with Combat *V* that read,

For heroic service as Commanding Officer on the USS NEHENTA BAY during a series of fueling operations in support of the THIRD Fleet attacks on enemy Japanese forces in the South China Sea, January 9 to 20, 1945. Operating as a part of a screening force in a high speed fueling and plane replacement group, Captain McDonnell directed his ship in supporting the first penetration of the South China Sea by United States surface forces since the early days of the war. Although the success of the mission was endangered on several occasions by hostile aerial attacks in which three Japanese planes were destroyed by Combat Air Patrol over the fueling groups and others shot down outside of visual range of the formation, Rear Admiral McDonnell (then Captain) by his professional skill, initiative and leadership, effectively executed the many complex details of his assignment not only to insure the safety of his ship, but also to render the logistic support essential to the success of the operation. His conduct throughout this period was in keeping with the highest traditions of the United States Naval Service.

After the Battle of the South China Seas, the damaged ship was ordered back to San Diego for repairs and resupply. Once completed, the escort carrier returned to Hawaii and later Guam to train and qualify replacement aviators for the war's final push.

In May of 1945, the *Nehenta Bay* was ordered to Ulithi Island to prepare for the invasion of Okinawa. It was during the Battle of Okinawa that the ship came under attack numerous times. On June 7, she was hit by two kamikazes and sustained heavy damage. Yet even these suicide attacks couldn't deter her from fulfilling her duty. She stayed in the fray and continued her great legacy of providing critical air support during one of the bloodiest battles of World War II. Under nearly constant attack by kamikazes and onshore batteries, the *Nehenta Bay* earned her seventh battle star of World War II, and her commander, Eddie McDonnell, received the Asiatic-Pacific Campaign Medal.

Eddie on board the USS *Nehenta Bay* at the Battle of Okinawa, 1945.

After the Battle of Okinawa, the ship continued its resupply and escort missions in support of the larger frontline aircraft carriers and onshore combatants. The *Nehenta Bay* was on a resupply and troop recovery mission in the Aleutian Islands when the war with Japan officially ended. Eddie and his ship were then ordered to change course and proceed to the northern islands of Japan. It was there in Mutsu Bay on September 6, 1945, that Eddie stood with another Medal of Honor recipient from Vera Cruz, Admiral Jack Fletcher, as he accepted the Japanese surrender of the islands of Honshu and Hokkaido. This was the same Admiral Fletcher who replaced a sick Bull Halsey and helped win the Battle of Midway.

Eddie McDonnell on board the USS *Nahenta Bay* at Mutsu Bay, Japan, 1945.

Eddie and the *Nehenta Bay* then joined Operation Magic Carpet. He spent the next few months transporting aircraft, troops, and surplus materials back to the United States. Upon his final return to the States, Eddie was relieved as the commander of the *Nehenta Bay* and named the special assistant to the flight pay board at the office of the deputy chief of Naval Operations in Washington, DC. He was relieved from active duty a short time later and returned to the active naval reserves. In December 1951, he was promoted to vice admiral and placed on the reserve retired list, thus ending the forty-three-year military career of the greatest naval aviator in American history.

Eddie turning over command USS *Nehenta Bay*, Pearl Harbor, 1945.

CHAPTER EIGHT

After Eddie was relieved from active duty at the end of 1945, he returned to his home in Mill Neck, New York, and resumed his career as an investment banker and senior partner at Hornblower & Weeks.

When Hornblower acquired Grayson M.P. Murphy & Co. in 1938, one of the company's priorities had been to gain an aviation expert and the board seats that Grayson Murphy had controlled. Hornblower & Weeks did this in order to increase their market presence and further influence the fledgling civilian aviation and air transportation industries. That expert came in the form of Edward McDonnell.

Eddie was recognized as the leading authority on aviation and airlines companies in general. Companies such as Pan American, United Airlines, Boeing, and Lockheed had all looked to Eddie for financing and guidance during their early formative years. That he was on the board of directors and a trusted advisor/financier to many of these companies would obviously give Hornblower a leg up on the competition.

But Eddie was never content to rest on his laurels. He was always looking for new opportunities, whether those companies were in commercial aviation, travel and tourism, or government defense contracts. Any well-managed company, regardless of the industry, that was looking to grow and increase its market share knew that

Eddie McDonnell, while always a tough sell, would be willing to listen.

One of those companies was Pepsi Cola. Pepsi was looked upon as the perpetual runner-up and poor stepchild of its Southern neighbor Coca-Cola. In 1938, Pepsi named Walter S. Mack president and placed him in charge of day-to-day operations. Mack served as both president and chairman from 1951 until he resigned in 1956.

Walter S. Mack was a big, rugged man, the grandson of an early Texas Ranger, and had graduated from Harvard in 1917. Upon graduation, he served on destroyers in the Atlantic during World War I. He was used to adversity and hard work. Risk-taking was the way he lived and later became his business philosophy.

After the war, Mack went to work for the Bedford Textile Mills. He was named president of the company in 1926. Approximately five years later, he left Bedford and became an investment banker in New York. Although he had heard of Eddie's exploits during World War I, it was not until 1931 that the two became friends.

Mack had built his reputation on finding troubled companies with good products but little capital. He would then provide that company with the necessary funds it needed in exchange for stock options and a say in that company's management. One such company was Loft's Candies.

Charles Guth was in charge at the Loft's candy chain, based in New York, when Mack discovered an old soda fountain syrup recipe and saw its potential. The syrup recipe was from a long-forgotten formula that had been part of the assets that Guth had purchased after the original Pepsi had gone bankrupt in the 1920s. The original Pepsi had been the brainchild of, and was invented by, a North Carolina pharmacist named Caleb Bradham in the late 1800s. Bradham, through a series of bad investments and a lack of true business acumen, had allowed Pepsi to sink into bankruptcy in 1923.

Mack and Charles Guth were interested in formulating a new cola syrup for Loft's Candies stores, many of which included soda fountains. He did this because industry giant Coca-Cola refused to grant him the discounts he felt his company deserved due to the volume it was purchasing. So, it was left up to Mack and Guth to either pay Coca-Cola or create its own soda syrup. They chose the latter.

Because both Coke and Pepsi were similar in taste, Mack understood that the best way to grow Pepsi was to take market share away from its rival. He had decided to add the word *cola* to Pepsi's name. Coke sued Pepsi, but lost the suit in the late 1930s. This was how the "Cola Wars" began.

Mack knew that he was the logical choice to lead Pepsi in its aggressive challenge of Coca-Cola. He knew how to market and distribute products from his experiences at Bedford Mills. But something else was needed for this new cola to really make a splash. As I stated earlier, Mack had gotten to know Eddie when they both were working as investment bankers/financiers in New York in the early 1930s. In 1938, Pepsi was looking for additional capital in order to finance the lawsuit and mount a serious challenge to its rival Coke. Mack contacted Eddie about securing that additional capital. Eddie not only saw Pepsi's potential, but he also helped Mack reconnect with some of his old friends in the Navy. This is how Pepsi become the soft drink of choice for the US Navy during World War II.

So, when Eddie rejoined the Pepsi's board just after World War II, it had already increased its market share through its contract with the Navy. It was fortunate that thousands of returning sailors now favored Pepsi over Coke. Therefore, it was up to Pepsi's management team to cultivate that relationship and further increase its popularity. Enter Alfred N. Steele.

Steele was the right man at the right time for Pepsi. After graduating from Northwestern University, Steele had joined Coca-Cola. He had worked his way up to vice president of marketing at Coca-Cola, so he was familiar with their strategies and secrets. He knew just how to develop a plan to combat Coke and further decrease its market share.

Steele helped reposition Pepsi by lowering its sugar content and making it taste even more like Coke. He worked tirelessly to introduce this new brand of cola into foreign markets and developing countries. Sales increased dramatically. So much, in fact, that he was named CEO in 1949. Steele, during his tenure until 1959, when he passed away, increased Pepsi sales by 300 percent. This was partly due to his newfound connection to Hollywood and its stars.

In 1955, Steele married Joan Crawford. Almost immediately, she became the face of Pepsi and its spokesperson. Pepsi was featured in several very popular films and developed advertising jingles that reminded people that there was a new drink in town. Pepsi also had several other advantages. It was well capitalized, and its board was comprised of members from many different industries, with many different skill sets. One of those men was Eddie McDonnell.

Eddie and Pepsi had another advantage that was still in its development stages at this time. Eddie's eldest daughter, Ann, had been divorced from her first husband, Oliver Grace, for several years when she met a tall, handsome Navy pilot from Washington State named Donald Kendall. Eddie took an immediate liking to the young man who looked much older due to his head of grayish, silver hair.

Eddie recognized many of the traits and strengths that he himself possessed—traits such as a strong work ethic, aggressive nature, and intelligence. My mother also thought that, because of Don's aviation background, he reminded Eddie of his son Edward Jr. Whatever the reason, Ann and Don were married after World War II.

Don Kendall joined Pepsi in 1947. Because of his father-in-law, Eddie, I always thought that Don had been handed the golden ticket to success. But this was not the case. Instead, Don joined Pepsi as a trainee in its New Rochelle, NY, plant. He started at the bottom and had to learn every aspect of the operation.

He rose quickly through the ranks due to his hard work and determination. He took every opportunity to listen and learn from Eddie. Betty would say that Don often credited his Navy training and service with instilling many important business practices. These practices included diversification, the importance of strong leadership, and the ability to look for opportunities outside your comfort zone.

As Alfred Steele had demonstrated, international expansion and adapting to changing market conditions were critical for Pepsi to grow and expand its market share. Over the next decade, Don worked his way up through the ranks of Pepsi until he became a vital member of its executive team.

But Eddie had seen something more in Don. He knew that, with the right opportunities, Don could make Pepsi the largest beverage company in the world. That opportunity came in 1959.

Don had accompanied his good friend, then Vice President Richard Nixon, on a trip to Moscow. It was a warm day and, after several hours of heated discussions with Nikita Khrushchev, Nixon and his advisors took a short break. It was during this break that Khrushchev noticed Nixon drinking a Pepsi that Don had given to him.

When asked, Don promptly handed a bottle of his "Capitalist Cola" to Mr. Khrushchev. The famous picture of Nixon, Khrushchev, and Kendall sharing a cold Pepsi was picked up by almost all the major news and wire services. Pepsi's expansion into the USSR and Soviet bloc nations initiated an international campaign and made Donald Kendall a star at Pepsi.

While it was fortunate for Pepsi to become the favored soft drink in the Soviet Union and Eastern Europe, there was still one major hurdle for Donald to overcome. The United States did not accept the Russian ruble as hard currency or legal tender in international financing. So, in order to complete the deal allowing Pepsi products to be sold in Russia, another form of currency had to be found. And that, my mother Betty explained, was how Stolichnaya vodka came to the US. She would often chuckle as she sipped on a Stoli martini, claiming the United States certainly got the better of that deal.

Another of the many fascinating stories Betty would tell was of the ongoing battles that Don "White Fang" Kendall had with his fellow board member Joan Crawford. "White Fang" was Joan's derogative pet name for Don. She had joined the Pepsi board when her fourth husband, Alfred Steele, had died in 1959. Steele had been elected chairman when Walter Mack decided to leave his leadership position at Pepsi. Steele was considered old school. He (and later his wife, Joan) felt that Pepsi should stick to the business it knew best, the soft-drink industry. Don had other ideas.

He wanted to expand into the new worlds of snack and fast foods. Why not have a Pepsi with your burger or chicken? Instead of a Coke, drink a Pepsi while munching on a bag of chips or pretzels. Don had met Herman Lay at a grocer's convention in 1963. By 1965, the two had agreed to merge Pepsi with Frito-Lay, and a new food and beverage giant, PepsiCo, was born.

Throughout the next few years, Don and PepsiCo managed to acquire Pizza Hut, Taco Bell, and Kentucky Fried Chicken. He did this while slowly forcing his rival at Pepsi, Joan Crawford, off the Pepsi board, and excluding her from the much larger PepsiCo's board to which he was elected chairman in 1971. The heated discussions and boardroom arguments at Pepsi were legendary. And yes, Ms. Crawford was an even bigger "bitch" in the boardroom then she was on a movie set, or when parenting her poor adopted daughter. She was truly *Mommie Dearest* and was detested by most of Pepsi's board, including my grandfather Eddie McDonnell.

Many of Eddie's business successes were due to his ability to inspire confidence and maintain long-term relationships. These relationships were usually based on the intense feelings of loyalty that each participant had for the other. According to my mother, this idea of loyalty was deeply instilled by Eddie's family at a very young age. It was further reinforced by his time spent at Annapolis. Loyalty and the duty that came with it were the cornerstones of the discipline expected and demanded at the United States Naval Academy.

One example of this loyalty and trust built over time was Eddie's relationship with John D. Hertz. Hertz was an invited participant on the Millionaires Flight of the Hindenburg. Although Eddie knew John Hertz in passing, it wasn't until the 1936 flight that the gentleman got to really know each other and become fast friends.

Hertz was the founder and president of the Yellow Truck and Coach manufacturing company. In 1923, John Hertz became interested in and purchased the Chicago based Rent-A-Car Inc. from Walter Jacobs. Hertz had recognized the need for businessmen and other travelers to have access to an automobile without having to wait for a taxi or pay the high costs of a limo and driver. He renamed the company the Hertz Drive-Ur-Self System and sold it three years later to General Motors.

It was in 1953 that John Hertz, who at the time was a partner in Lehman Brothers, approached Eddie with the idea of buying back the rental car and truck enterprise from General Motors. They put together a financing package and the Hertz Rent-A-Car Company was born. As Betty pointed out later, Hertz's connection to Yellow Cab of Chicago and the Yellow Truck and Coach companies was the reason that Hertz's logo was yellow (and because they wanted to differentiate themselves from Hertz, Avis car rental chose red).

But connections and mergers extended beyond just business. Often, they were of a personal nature. One story in particular illustrates this extremely well.

Betty referred to this story as the "the merger through marriage tale." It was shortly after the war when one of Eddie's nieces, and my mother's closest cousin, Austine McDonnell, "merged through marriage" two of America's great families. Austine had been working for a newspaper in New York when she met and fell in love with a member of the Hearst family. She and William Randolph Hearst Jr. married in 1948. Their union produced two delightful and extremely successful sons, William III and John Augustine "Austin" Hearst.

Austin and I do share one other thing in common. My mother was his godmother, and his mother was mine. While I didn't get to know Austine Hearst (or "Bootsie" as she was called) well, I do remember that she never missed my birthday or Christmas. I always received a gift and card with well wishes enclosed. Not bad for one of the truly "grande dames" of her day!

CHAPTER NINE

In addition to earning a substantial living, Eddie's business ventures allowed him to indulge in his other great passions—hunting and fishing. Many of Betty's favorite tales dealt with this subject. They were also my favorite stories to listen to and dream about. If only I could have joined him on one of these adventures, it would have been a memory that lasted a lifetime. Sometimes, in telling these stories, the dates of his exploits would change, get confused, or become a little muddled, but the outcomes were never in doubt. As his trophy rooms could attest, Eddie was an extremely skilled sportsman who loved to indulge his passions.

Eddie, Helen, and fellow board members and wives, Paris, 1954.
Eddie left for Norway soon after.

And indulge them he did. One of my favorite stories was about Christmas gifts that my grandmother Helen and Eddie were going to give each other. I believe it was around 1937, when my grandfather announced to his wife that for Christmas, he was going to purchase a fine, custom Browning double-barreled 12-gauge shotgun for her from Belgium. Nana McDonnell was not very pleased. But being a good sport, the consummate manipulator, and wanting to appease her husband, she agreed to the shotgun.

Several days later, she announced at dinner that Eddie was going to love the gift she had picked out for him. She had called one of her favorite furriers in New York and purchased a beautiful, full length Chinchilla coat. It might be a little small, she told him, but with some proper tailoring, it should fit. After a good chuckle, they both agreed to switch the tags on the gift boxes and enjoyed a wonderful Christmas!

Eddie and Helen at home in Mill Neck, New York, Christmas, 1943.

Many of the great sportsmen in the early twentieth century would indulge their passions while on business trips. John Houston, an acquaintance of Eddie's, would often hunt or fish while on location directing a film.

William Holden, a fellow hunter and another friend of Eddie's, would often choose his movie roles based on where the filming was to take place. Several of his movies were set in Africa, where he and my grandfather were instrumental in helping to fund and set aside vast areas of land for game preserves.

Hemingway's passion for fishing lead him to the Florida Keys, where he used his celebrity to help create a cluster of offshore reefs and other fishing habitats that were critical in the conservation of numerous species of fish, coral, and other sea life.

True hunters and sportsmen are often the prime motivators in the conservation movement. They provide the impetus and knowledge necessary for the preservation of wildlife and the land or water on which they depend. They understand that careful game management is essential in conservation and the protection of the hunted species. When your passion is hunting or fishing, it just doesn't make sense to damage or overuse the areas that you depend upon.

Men such as Holden, Hemingway, Houston, and my grandfather were responsible for preserving and maintaining huge plots of land, freshwater areas, and oceans for the benefit of the native wildlife. The indigenous populations that earn a living off tourism, hunting, and fishing often lack the funds or knowledge to fight the bureaucracies or burdensome regulations that threaten those habitats. It takes deep pockets, connections, and a willingness to work with the locals to preserve these habitats. But first and foremost, these habitats need to be located and identified. Sportsmen are most often the ones who bring the areas in need of conservation into the public consciousness. This is why Eddie rarely missed an opportunity to travel with other Pan Am board member on their sorties to explore new routes or destinations in Africa, South America, or Asia. Several of my favorite photos show Eddie with the airline's executive board posing for photos in front of a large, older commercial airliner. All the men are in suits, usually wearing hats, and carrying briefcases. The ladies are dressed to the nines, and everyone, including my grandfather, seem quite serious. The one item in all these pictures that seems out of place is the fly-fishing rod case, or cases, in my grandfather's hand.

He absolutely refused to miss an opportunity to wet a line. Salt water or fresh water, only the size and number of the cases seemed to change. As Betty liked to point out, apparently where her father was concerned, the slogan, "Don't leave home without it," has more to do with fly rods than credit cards.

Eddie with his favorite salt water fly rods, Hawaii, 1956.

It was always the stories of my grandfather's exploits while hunting or fishing that brought out the brightest twinkle in my mother's eyes. I knew that the challenges and exploits of his youth, whether on the playing fields, in battle, or testing new aircraft, helped make Eddie what we would call an "adrenalin junkie" in this day and age.

As I discovered at a very young age, this adrenalin junkie trait runs deep within the McDonnell and Barry DNA. We spend much of our early lives searching for adventure. Whether it is the thrill of extreme skiing, the danger of intense class four and five whitewater, or the challenge of high-altitude mountaineering, we did it. Often, it was the exhilaration of a brisk morning riding after a large pack of hounds as they chase their quarry over the open hills and grassy valleys of central

Colorado. Our family's passion for testing the human limits never ends.

But as we get older, hopefully the wisdom that comes with this process translates into common sense. Such was the case for my grandfather. His passion for adventure morphed into new pursuits.

Hunting and fishing had always been enjoyed by the admiral. Growing up on the Chesapeake Bay in Maryland had allowed all the McDonnell brothers an opportunity to hunt and fish. They each became masters of the craft and pursued their chosen sport with an unrivaled exuberance.

Fortunately for Eddie, his ability to travel and afford these pursuits was enhanced by his position as an investment banker. Whether it was in Alaska hunting for Kodiak and polar bears, in the jungles of South America stalking the elusive jaguar, or catching salmon in Norway, Eddie knew the areas that were both productive and in need of protection. He was at the forefront of the conservation movement and the preservation of these fragile native habitats. There are only so many pristine locations where a sportsman can truly indulge his or her passions. Eddie knew this and further realized the great responsibility he had toward the areas where he harvested much of his wild game and fish.

Eddie also believed that when hunting, using traditional methods, such as a spear or bow and arrow, was almost always the preferred method. This was demonstrated quite thoroughly in one of the most remarkable tales my mother told me when I was very young. Most of these stories started out the same way; "Your grandfather was on one of his many fact-finding trips as an investment banker and director for Pan American Airlines . . ."

One such adventure occurred in the Amazon River basin of Peru and Brazil. On this trip, Eddie was to conclude his business in Sao Paulo, Brazil, and then meet up with his brother and frequent hunting companion, John McDonnell. The brothers would fly to the launch point, then spend a few days fishing while traveling up the Amazon toward their destination.

They had decided to search deep in the Brazilian jungle to hunt for the elusive jaguar. It took the brothers well over a week to travel upstream into the area of the Amazon basin nearly halfway to the Peruvian border, where the hunt was to take place.

It is important to remember that the South American jaguar is the largest and most feared predator on the continent. Its strength, speed, claws, and powerful jaws make it lethal. Its acute senses, stealth, and heavily camouflaged coat make it extremely difficult to spot, let alone hunt. Often while hunting the big cat, it will hide and lay in wait for its stalker. The jaguar is well known for turning its predator into prey, and its prey into its next meal. Combine this with Eddie's desire to take this large cat in the traditional method, and let the story unfold.

The traditional native method for hunting jaguar is with a javelin, a long, usually eight- to ten-foot spear, with points at both ends. Because the jaguar is a nocturnal hunter, the hunt occurs at night and uses a bait to lure in the big cat. The bait in this case was a staked goat.

The theory goes that the goat will draw the jaguar into the killing area, while the hunter stands off in the shadows, trying to remain as still and quiet as possible. Once the cat is charging and fully committed to the bawling bait, the hunter steps from the shadows. The jaguar, seeing the human as a greater threat, will often change course and charge its new prey.

When the cat does this, the hunter plants one end of the javelin into the ground. The hunter then secures the planted end with his or her foot. They do this while hoping that the leaping predator impales itself on the spear, striking a vital organ and killing it instantly.

That, once again, is the perfect scenario. But being in the middle of the Amazon basin and dealing with an extremely dangerous predator—plans rarely go perfectly or even smoothly. Such was the case on this hunt. Apparently, Eddie's guides had staked out the only deaf, dumb, and blind goat in the entire region. When the jaguar charged, the goat didn't react in the slightest. As it leaped toward the staked goat's back, there was not a sound or indication of its impending doom.

About the only indication that the huge cat was even present was the awful sound of cracking bones as the goat's neck was crushed by the cat's powerful jaws. After a slight struggle, the goat lay still.

One of the guides, who had been hidden in the brush near Eddie, made a mistake and moved toward the now lifeless goat. Seeing the guide's movement, Eddie stepped out into the open, still carrying the long straight spear.

Startled, by the guide's and my grandfather's movements, the jaguar, with its kill still secure within its great maw, now focused on Eddie and company. After tossing the goat aside like a rag doll—and completely without warning—the cat leapt at the guide. Clamping down on the guide's leg, the big cat began dragging its terrified, screaming victim toward the dense jungle. Seeing the man flailing, without any thought or concern for his own safety, Eddie picked up a small rock and threw it at the animal's head. The rock struck the jaguar between its eye and ear. Infuriated, the cat released the guide's leg, turned, and charged my grandfather.

The snarling cat closed rapidly, and from about fifteen feet, leapt at Eddie. There was barely enough time for Eddie to swing his javelin into place and anchor it with his foot before the huge cat would be upon him. With claws extended, and mouth opened for the kill, the cat impaled itself on the long spear. The killing end of the javelin penetrated the jaguar's heart. The beast died almost instantly and landed squarely on the chest of the now flattened and extremely shaken investment banker. This huge male cat weighed well over 200 pounds and was nearly ten feet long from the tip of its nose to the tip of its tail.

The next week was spent recovering from the hunt, tending to the wounded guide, and fishing for giant tambaqui and tucunaré (peacock bass) while traveling back down the Amazon River toward the take-out point.

Another one of Betty's more remarkable tales involved one of my grandfather's many African safaris. Again, his brother and my great-uncle, John McDonnell, went with him. Even though I had heard the story from my mother on many occasions, it wasn't until John regaled our family with this same tale that I began to really understand the extreme danger of that safari. I can still hear the old gentleman's voice as I sat on the edge of the large leather sofa in the study of his Warrenton farm.

The ability to tell a truly remarkable tale using the kind of vivid descriptions that could hold the attention of a ten-year-old boy was one of the many gifts that the McDonnell family was blessed with.

This hunt took place about two years after the South American jaguar hunt but was certainly just as memorable. One thing that is very important to remember is that these hunts took many months—if not years—to plan. This trip was one of the latter. The sites were selected based upon the type of quarry to be hunted. This safari was to take place in South Africa. After contacting the local guides, it was decided to go after at least one of the "big five," Africa's most feared and hunted big game—the elephant, the rhinoceros, the lion, the leopard, and the water buffalo. In addition to hunting kudu, gemsbok, and sable antelope, Eddie's focus was on the water buffalo—Cape buffalo, to be specific.

Eddie had yet to be successful in his quest for this trophy and knew that his collection wouldn't be complete without it. Many hunters and sportsmen consider the Cape buffalo to be the most dangerous of all African big game. There have been many stories of a wounded buffalo lying in wait to ambush the offending hunter.

Prior to any trip that involved a stop in Europe, and Paris in particular, one chore above all others had to be taken care of—where, when, and what to eat during their layover. This incredibly time-consuming chore consisted of selecting a dining location, and then planning the menu. John and Eddie spent many hours arguing about what they were going to eat during their stay in Paris.

The restaurants were selected. Was it Maxim's or Le Dome the first night? Each course was meticulously laid out and planned. As Betty would explain years later, selection of each course or meal, as well as the proper wine to serve, was an art form, a strategy. These brothers would insist on different selections, argue, then compromise, for hours at a time. Each brother suggesting an appetizer while the other came up with something even more outlandish.

It was like a chess match or a fencing bout. No, it was as though these two senior military officers were conducting war games, and it was just that serious. Each would know what the other was thinking and would have to plan two or three moves or courses ahead.

Their wives, my grandmother Helen and my great-aunt Dorothy, would sit back in amusement, truly amazed and often frustrated as these two antagonists would parry and thrust. My Nana once told me that these two could decide where and what they were going to hunt in a matter of hours. But the menu selections could take weeks or even months to decide. But I digress.

These subspecies of water buffalo can stand five to six feet at the shoulder and weigh over a ton. Their poor eyesight means that they rely on their keen sense of hearing and smell to locate danger. They are fast, agile, and usually equipped with a tremendous set of horns—some set over seven feet from tip to tip.

One such bull was the target of a hunt by my grandfather. Typically, these huge animals lived together in small herds, with the alpha bull leading a subgroup of cows and calves. The massive old bull that Eddie was stalking was more of a solitary animal and had just one huge, older cow with him. My great-uncle John had taken a slightly smaller bull several days earlier and decided to sit out and relax that day while Eddie hunted.

After several hours of hiking, the guide, my grandfather, and a couple of porters were standing at the edge of some exceptionally tall grasses. All the members of the hunting party were extremely apprehensive about following this pair of trophy specimens into the tall, bushy grasses where the beasts had lumbered to graze.

But the challenge, bragging rights over his brother John, and a chance at a possible record trophy bull were just too many great temptations for my grandfather to withstand. When the lead guide refused to enter the tall grass, Eddie's hubris virtually forced him to foolishly venture on alone. After hacking a short distance through the dense brush with a machete, Eddie came upon a wide game trail that had been flattened by much use over time. Its tall, dense, grassy walls were at least eight feet in height. The trail was over ten feet wide and several hundred yards long. It was obviously a trail that had been walked on and grazed upon by buffalo, and possibly elephants or rhinos.

As Eddie entered the game trail, he heard a loud snort and the pounding thud of a hoof on the hardened ground. He also remembered the distinct sweet smell of fresh manure, as well as the sour smell of animal sweat.

When he looked to his right, less than fifty yards away was the enormous bull Cape buffalo that he had been stalking. Unfortunately, upon hearing another loud snort and looking to his left, he discovered the bull's mate approximately the same distance in the opposite direction. Both were facing him and, from the looks and sound of things, both were preparing to simultaneously charge. Eddie was an expert marksman, but at that moment, he realized what a fool he had been to continue into the tall grass alone, without a guide or at least a second shooter, like his brother John.

As he told my mother Betty several years later while recounting this adventure to her, "Seeing those two water buffalos staring at me from opposite directions made me realize that I was now the hunted and not the hunter. They had turned me from predator into prey. I knew what real terror felt like. For one of the few times in my life, I could taste fear!"

I thought of what my grandfather had said, and it made me realize that true fear or an absolute feeling of terror is almost always self-inflicted.

Here was a man who stood as a target on the roof of a Vera Cruz hotel under constant enemy fire. A man who had launched himself off a battleship gun turret, with a forty-four-foot ramp, in an airplane made of wood and canvas. A man who had flown over the Alps in an aircraft that probably should not have left the ground. One who had seen and tasted combat in two world wars. Yet, this encounter was one of the few times that he had truly felt a foreboding sense of his own mortality. And this strange feeling of impending doom was due entirely to his own poor judgment and decision to walk forward into the high brush alone.

But why, after all the life-threatening situations he had experienced, did this one stand out?

When I asked Betty, she explained it this way. In nearly all his close encounters with death, it was Eddie versus another man or man-made object. These situations, he could plan for and overcome by his own innate intelligence and courage. This encounter was something he hadn't prepared for or even thought about. It was him versus the raw power of nature. It could and had to be overcome, but he had far less control over the outcome. This lack of situational control was what my grandfather truly feared.

Eddie knew from experience that there was no way he could aim, shoot, strike, and kill the first buffalo, then spin, while possibly reloading, aim, and stop the second animal. Certainly not at this close range.

He had only seconds to determine which animal to take first. That decision was made for him when, suddenly, the enormous bull, enraged by the scent of an unknown foe, charged.

Ignoring the cow, Eddie leveled his Holland and Hollands double rifle and fired. Luckily, his aim was on target, and the heavy .375 caliber slug knocked the bull to its knees just a few yards from Eddie's feet.

Hearing the awful sound of the charging cow, Eddie turned just in time to see the enraged animal, running at full speed and less than twenty feet from where he was standing, swerve and disappear into the tall grasses on the side of the trail.

His only explanation was that the charging cow, startled from the loud noise of the rifle shot, seeing her mate crumble to the ground, had fled in fear. But this was not the end of the story.

After the kill, the guides and porters prepared the animal to be transported back to a nearby village. The head and horns were removed and set aside for my grandfather as a trophy. The rest of the carcass was butchered and packed to be given to a local tribe. Sometime during the processing of the buffalo, the young guide who had refused to go into the tall grass with Eddie had slipped away. Apparently, the lead guide on this safari had criticized him and questioned his bravery and manhood. The subordinate guide had left his rifle and wandered away while the rest of the group, including the porters, finished their work and left for the village.

When the young guide still had not returned after several hours, a couple of his fellow guides went looking for him. They returned shortly after dark and reported that they had not seen any trace of the young man. The next day, the search area was expanded, but there was still no sign of the young guide.

On the third day, around noon, they located the young man. Unfortunately, he was dead, found up in a small tree about four miles from where the large bull had been killed, and about eight miles from the village. He had climbed up onto the highest and largest branch that would support his weight. The branch was about eight or nine feet off the ground. Fearing that he would fall, the young man had tied himself to the trunk.

It was obvious that something had forced or chased him into the tree and kept the terrified young man from climbing down. Something extremely large and apparently dangerous. The search party could see many tracks surrounding and encircling the tree, along with a rather large puddle of dried blood near the tree's base. But there was something else quite disturbing about the scene. The trunk, just a few feet under the branch where the body of the young guide was, had many marks or scars on it. The bark of the tree had been almost completely scraped off and removed just below the hanging foot of the young man.

But they were not claw marks like the kind a lion or leopard would make. These were the scrape marks of a hoofed animal. Upon closer examination of the body, the lead guide made an educated guess as to what had happened. The young guide had died from blood loss. The bottom of his right foot was nearly devoid of skin and had several small puncture marks on it. It was determined that the young man had literally bled to death from the sole of his right foot.

But how did this happen? The lead guide explained that the tracks surrounding the tree belonged to an old, quite large Cape buffalo, probably a female. Although the buffalo couldn't reach the young man while standing on the ground on all fours, it could reach the level of his foot if it stood on its rear legs and balanced it front leg on the trunk. Then, as the young man tired and his legs grew heavy, the buffalo would lick at his foot with its sandpaper-like tongue and poke at it with the tips of its extremely rough and pointed horns. Apparently, this went on for several days, and once the blood started to flow, the young man's fate was sealed.

After removing the body from the tree, the searchers were returning it to the village for burial. They had gone less than a mile from the tree, when, to their amazement and absolute horror, they saw the dead bull's mate watching them from a distance.

As my mother so eloquently put it, "Forget cold. This buffalo's revenge was best served very warm, indeed."

As we have seen in the Pan American photos, it was obvious that fishing, both salt water and fresh water, was another of Eddie's great passions. It was while enjoying this pursuit that he met and became friends with some of the most famous and influential people of his time.

On one of his frequent business trips to Cuba in the late 1940s, he was introduced through a mutual friend to the owner of the *Pilar,* writer Ernest Hemingway. The *Pilar* was one of the first boats designed with a specific function in mind. Hemingway wanted to catch large trophy saltwater game fish. Giant tuna, huge marlin, and sailfish were his targets. Most boats at that time were small open skiffs, larger commercial fishing vessels or pleasure boats used for water skiing or sailing. But Hemingway wanted something that could ride out the storms and rough waters of the Florida Straits. Often spending a night or two at sea was necessary, so the boat needed to be dry and comfortable.

He accomplished this when he purchased a thirty-eight-foot cabin cruiser from Wheeler Shipbuilding in Brooklyn, New York, in 1934. He had spent over $7,000 on the craft and had outfitted it with a fighting chair, outriggers, a flying bridge, and other features designed to his personal fishing specifications. Eddie had heard about this boat and arranged through a mutual friend to see it and go fishing with the author.

Betty didn't recall many of the details from the fishing excursion, except that both men were extremely competitive and that her father found it quite odd that Hemingway carried a Thompson submachine gun on board to ward off sharks after a catch. Her father was disappointed that Hemingway caught both the largest dorado and marlin of the trip. But Eddie was quick to recall that he caught the only sailfish, which weighed over ninety pounds. This same fish was later prominently displayed at his home in Hobe Sound, Florida.

The only other detail that Betty remembered was that both men had felt little or no pain after the plentiful libations were served on the ride back to the marina. Ah, the life of the gentleman sportsman!

Eddie had become enamored with the *Pilar.* The idea of a high speed, dry, and stable fishing platform set his mind racing. In fact, upon returning to his winter home in Hobe Sound/Jupiter Island, Florida, he started to research and design this type of vessel for himself. He visited numerous small boat builders and marinas looking for either the right boat to customize or a manufacturer to construct a sportfisherman for him.

He found that someone in Curtis "Curt" Whiticar. Curt had grown up in the East Coast fishing industry. His father, Addison, or "Captain Add" as he was known, was a commercial fisherman who moved to Stuart, Florida, in 1917. When large-scale fishing operations reduced the fish populations, Captain Add started using his boat to charter fishing excursions for the well-heeled snowbirds of Florida's "Treasure Coast."

While still in his early twenties, Curt designed and built a thirty-three-foot fishing boat that was able to handle the challenging waters on the inlets of Florida's Atlantic coast. In 1938, Curt built with his father a thirty-eight-foot craft called the *Gannet*, which was exactly the type of fishing platform that Eddie had envisioned. So, after many discussions and much deliberation, Eddie chose Curt to build his boat. Curt's solid reputation as a boatyard owner and his understanding of local water conditions made him the ideal choice. Eddie's proximity to Stuart enabled him to watch the progress of the build whenever he was visiting Hobe Sound. Eddie would have a craft that not only rivaled the *Pilar* but surpassed it due to new materials and construction techniques. It would also cost considerably more than the $7,400 that Hemingway had spent.

Eddie justified the expense by repeating one of his favorite sayings: "I'm very easy to please; I'm always satisfied with the best!" It was decided that the boat would be thirty-eight-feet in length, with a deep V-hull shape that could handle the large swells and often treacherous waves of the Jupiter Inlet. It also had to be dry and comfortable for guests such as his wife, daughters, and grandchildren. This, according to Betty, was one of her father's two great boating joys. The other, due to the maintenance costs, was when he sold his beloved sportfisherman.

My mother Betty with her father Eddie on his Whiticar sportsfisherman.

As a child, I was fortunate enough to go out deep-sea fishing with my family and Curt Whitcar on one of his boats. We caught many dorado, some large barracuda, and several sailfish.

One of the remarkable memories of this trip was when my sister Susan caught and released a rather young sailfish with a bent bill. Captain Curt told my father that this was the first sailfish he had ever seen with such a pronounced curve in its bill. This was one of the many wonderful childhood memories I have of fishing off Hobe Sound.

Another of my mother's favorite fish tales involved salmon fishing in Norway. It was several years after the end of World War II, and Betty would usually begin this story by reminding me that you don't fish for and catch salmon, you "kill" them. She would then regale me with the story of the "Norwegian salmon killing leases" on the Tana River in Finnmark, Norway.

Eddie relaxing at his Tana river lodge, 1954.

According to the story, there were two private leases that could last for several weeks up to the entire season. Each lease encompassed several miles of exclusive river access and came complete with a guide and lodge. The lodges were extremely luxurious and would never have been described as rustic. Each lodge also came equipped with a complete staff, if required by the lessee. The upper tract had a much newer and larger lodge, but the lower tract had much better fishing. My grandfather, always the fisherman, chose the lower tract.

Eddie with several freshly caught Tana River salmon, 1954.

Early in the salmon killing season, he was contacted by a staff member from the party who had leased the upper tract. The man, with a decidedly British accent, wanted to know if it would be possible if his employer and several guests could fish on the lower tract on occasion. Eddie and my grandmother Helen agreed, but they were amused that this man's employer wished to remain anonymous. They also found it strange that he was not Norwegian like the maids and chef at their lodge.

Imagine my grandparents' surprise when, about a week later, several Land Rovers pulled up, and out popped Prince Phillip and his wife, Elizabeth II. They were accompanied by another couple and immediately started asking questions about which fly to use, where the best holes were, and so forth.

This was how Eddie and my grandmother were introduced to the members of the British Royal Family. They remained friends for many years, and in fact, Queen Elizabeth, upon hearing of the death of my grandfather, sent a lovely condolence note to my grandmother.

I guess it is true, you meet all the best and most interesting people with a fishing rod in your hand.

Eddie and Helen McDonnell on the Tana River, 1954.

CHAPTER TEN

Betty would often grin, chuckle, or just flat out laugh while telling stories of her father and his family. My father and sister would hear us in the family room and know that we were locked into storytelling mode. Her memories of him, as well as her aunts, uncles, and brother, brought her joy, happiness, and a truly lasting sense of peace. She loved reconnecting with these memories, for they were among the best and most important ones in her life.

She knew how important these stories were to me as well. Through this oral tradition, I was able to learn about, and in a strange way also connect with, these fascinating and heroic characters from our past. I remember many of these characters from meeting them as a child. Uncles Francis and John, my Aunt Kathleen, and Bootsie Hearst all come to mind. But my memories are of when they were older. They were, of course, still interesting and full of fun, but they were in the twilight of their lives.

It was hard to imagine my eighty-year-old uncle John astride his thoroughbred hunter Tycos charging across the meadows and hedgerows of Virginia on a frosty and chill November morning. Or my aunt Kathleen climbing the stairs of the Alhambra or playing backgammon and drinking into the wee hours of the night in Spain. These people were too old for that. Yet, when hearing of their exploits from a master storyteller like my mother, they came to life. I could see Eddie and my extended family in their younger years.

This tale of my grandfather does, indeed, come to an end, just as the stories of each of us must reach the same inevitable conclusion. Some are more sudden. Some are more tragic. And some leave us wondering *what if.*

I used to think about what would've happened if my uncle Edward Jr. had lived past twenty-three years of age. Would he have taken me fishing and hunting? What impact would he have had on me as a child, teenager, and adult? And what about my grandfather Eddie? I know, judging by how he loved and treated his other grandchildren, that I would have enjoyed being with him. Possibly spending time hunting and fishing with my father, uncle, and him. But I'll never know.

Eddie on a hunting and fishing trip in Alaska, 1952.

I do know that the sudden and tragic end to this remarkable man's life was one of the most difficult times that my mother ever had to experience.

In fact, the only time that I did not see Betty smile when speaking of her father was when she spoke of that fateful night in January of 1960, when he was killed.

Like most fathers, Eddie had a tremendous impact on his daughter's life. But there was something else about their relationship that was even more startling. She was like her father in almost every way. Not with his military exploits nor heroics, but in the way she lived and enjoyed her life.

Both were committed to truly living. They wanted to experience all the wonders this world could offer. Travel, meeting interesting people, and taking the calculated risks that often bring the greatest rewards. That's what these two were about!

I often thought that she loved her father more than any other man in her life. I could never understand why she held such a special place in her heart until I asked my father, Arthur, about it. His explanation was quite simple and holds true in the relationship I have with my daughter Eva. Certain men hold women in very high esteem. One of the offshoots of this is that we tend to look at and treat our daughters differently. Our daughters sense that they are special and know that they are loved because of this special treatment. We spoil, protect, and cherish them in a way we never could with our sons. It is because of this special relationship with our girls that they reciprocate and often tend to look at their fathers through rose-colored glasses. Such was the relationship between my father and sister Susan. My wife, Renee, and her grandfather had this bond as well. So too was the relationship between my mother and her father. But there was more to it.

Betty was a mischievous child. She would get into trouble and, when confronted, would always accept both the responsibility and consequences. She would often talk back to her parents and seldom back down from a confrontation with her older sister or younger brother.

This behavior, while frustrating to her father, also endeared her to him. She had spunk. She had guts. She was sassy and full of adventure. In other words, she was the female version of Eddie. And he loved her for it.

And that was what made their relationship so remarkable. Yes, they were father and daughter, but they were also kindred spirits. They were friends, had the same ribald sense of humor, and most importantly, they held each other in very high regard.

Now, as I reflect on these stories, I can better understand why Betty would speak almost reverently of her father. This also helps us understand why she went from absolute joy to abject misery in the short span of a few weeks. Everything changed on January 6, 1960.

I was born on December 17, 1959. My mother was a nineteen-year-old student and aspiring model who became enamored with a young Argentinian law student attending Georgetown University. Having been raised a strict Catholic, abortion was not an option for her. Her parents insisted that she have the baby and immediately give it up for adoption through the Barker Foundation in Washington, DC. This foundation had the reputation of being the go-to place for the daughters of wealthy families to have their babies placed with other wealthy families in a most discrete manner.

I was the son that Betty and Arthur Barry couldn't have on their own because of differing Rh factors. Betty and Arthur had conceived four children, but tragically, none survived past birth. They had resigned themselves to the fact that the only way they were going to have children was through adoption.

In 1956, they got their wish and adopted a beautiful baby girl whom they named Susan Campbell Barry. Though unusual, after several years, they were granted a second adoption through Barker's. I was that second child. After my birth in December, my adoptive parents still had to wait for about three weeks before I could be permanently placed in their home. I was named Edward Orrick McDonnell Barry, after both Betty's father and brother.

As we know, Betty absolutely adored her father and had an extremely close relationship to her brother "Boy." When he was shot down over the Mediterranean Sea near Tunisia, a very important part of her life was lost. Her brother, the male connection to her father, was gone.

She looked upon me as a possible new connection or link to her father. She had finally given him a grandson. She knew that, as he aged, she would have more opportunities and a new, very important reason to spend time with him. That reason was me.

Prior to leaving for Frankfurt, Germany, for my father Arthur's next judge advocate posting, the family had scheduled a trip to introduce me to my grandfather. We were to fly down to his winter home in Hobe Sound, Florida, after I was permanently placed with my parents on January 9, 1960. They had wanted to say goodbye to Helen and Eddie and spend several weeks relaxing in the sun. This would also give my parents' furniture, cloths, and automobile time to reach Germany prior to our arrival there.

On the evening of January 5, 1960, Edward O. McDonnell was scheduled to leave New York's Idlewild International Airport on board a National Airlines flight bound for Miami. He had an important business meeting early in the morning and had scheduled a limousine that would drive him the two-plus hours north to his home on Jupiter Island and the town of Hobe Sound.

Unfortunately, the Boeing 707 jet that was scheduled to fly developed a crack in the windshield, which had to be repaired prior to flying again. The only other National planes that were available were smaller and older propeller-driven aircraft. It would take two of these planes to accommodate all the scheduled passengers who had been booked on the much larger Boeing jet. Eddie was booked on the first of the two flights that would leave later that night.

A few minutes prior to boarding the first substitute plane, my grandfather heard that a late arriving female passenger who was expecting her first child had been scheduled on the second flight that wasn't leaving until later that evening.

The young lady was quite concerned that the second, later flight might cause her to miss her connecting flight in Miami. Gallant as ever, Eddie volunteered to give up his seat and take the second flight. The second flight was aboard a DC-6, National flight 2511, and it was scheduled to leave New York about two hours later. This gentlemanly decision would prove fatal.

Early on the morning of January 6, approximately two hours into the National Airlines flight, an explosive device was detonated inside the cabin of the aircraft under the right wing of the plane. The right wing and engine having been lost, the DC-6 rapidly lost altitude. The aircraft disintegrated partially while still in the air and completely upon impact. The remaining parts of the plane were scattered over a wide area outside of the town of Bolivia, North Carolina.

All twenty-nine passengers and five crew members were killed. All the bodies but one were found near the main parts of the wreckage. One of the few bodies left nearly intact was that of Admiral Edward McDonnell, still strapped into his seat.

I can't imagine what those last few minutes must have been like for my grandfather and the other passengers. I am sure that, due to the lateness of the hour, many of them were asleep or dozing.

Then, suddenly and without warning, a loud explosion, slightly center forward and to the right side of the aircraft, allowed a blast of frigid night air into the plane. Some may have screamed as one of the other passengers was dismembered and sucked out of the DC-6. Others looked on in horror, and the right wing, with its engine engulfed in flames, was slowly torn from the now falling aircraft.

I'm sure that many were praying, some were screaming in terror, while others hugged and clutched their loved ones or even the stranger in the seat next to them. What thoughts were racing through their minds as the plane slowly banked and dove nose first toward its inevitable meeting with the hard ground nearly eighteen thousand feet below? Many thought of family or the loved ones they would never see again. Some might have just stared straight ahead waiting for the end—while others held onto the slim and fading hope that they would be among the survivors of this terrible trauma.

I think that, after all the tales I heard about Eddie McDonnell, I know what his thoughts and responses were to these awful events that were happening in the early morning hours of January 6, 1960.

Eddie, one of the heroes of Vera Cruz, an adventure-seeking hunter and a survivor of numerous close calls during the early days of flight, was perplexed. He wondered if there was anything he could do to improve the chances of the passenger's survival. I'm sure that, at some point, he was very calm and reflecting on his life and loved ones. He may have been reassuring and trying to calm the other passengers near him. He might even have thought of rushing toward the cockpit and seeing if there was anything he could do to save the doomed aircraft. I can only hope that he was rendered unconscious or even killed by the initial blast and did not have to experience those terrible minutes while the DC-6 dove toward the coastal farmlands of North Carolina.

One thing I am most sure of is that, if he had been conscience, Admiral Edward McDonnell did not panic. He did not scream. And he most assuredly did not cry or weep. That was just not his way of responding to a crisis or dire, desperate situation. When he determined that all was lost, he probably just sat back, took a deep breath, and waited. Simply hoping that he would soon be reunited with his beloved son, Boy, whom he lost those many years ago.

Although never proven, an investigation pointed to another passenger, Julian Frank, as the man who brought the bomb on board the aircraft. Frank, thirty-two years of age and a resident of Westport, Connecticut, was an attorney with a very questionable reputation. He was being investigated for charity fraud and the theft of monies from a mortgage lending scheme involving some of his investors and clients. He was facing the possible loss of his law license and considerable prison time, according to the Manhattan District Attorney's Office that had been investigating him for several months at the request of one of his clients.

So, as the authorities were collecting evidence and preparing to bring charges against him, Julian Frank launched a plan to take out nearly a million dollars in life insurance in the form of several large life insurance policies. He had done this over the course of several months and finalized the purchase of flight life insurance just prior to takeoff. According to the passenger check-in and baggage attendant, Frank seemed extremely nervous and upset. He had even gone so far as to say that he had a very bad feeling about the flight.

His plan, in theory, was simple. He would rig a bomb using dynamite and detonate it with a dry-cell battery while the plane was in flight. His seat in row seven was adjacent to the right wing on the DC-6 aircraft. He thought that if the plane were to disappear over the ocean on its way to Miami, FAA investigators might never know that the bomb he detonated had caused its destruction. His family would then be able to collect on the policy and no one would be the wiser.

His elaborate scheme had been foiled in part due to adverse weather conditions. National Airlines flight 2511 had to fly closer to the coast on its way toward Wilmington, North Carolina. Once over Wilmington, the plane would head out on the over-water leg of its flight to Miami. This meant that the plane was almost directly over the coastal city of Bolivia at an altitude of 18,000 feet.

Richard Randolph, a local farmer from the Bolivia area, reported hearing what sounded like an airplane engine cutting in and out at around 2:45 a.m., followed by a loud explosion a couple of minutes later. Another report cited that several other citizens of Bolivia heard a loud explosion at around 2:50 a.m. on the morning of January 6. Later that morning, as the sun began to rise, Randolph had to walk to the post office in Bolivia to use their telephone to report the crash to the proper authorities in town and at the Wilmington airport.

The plane went down in a field that Randolph owned several miles from the town of Bolivia. Some of the aircraft's other pieces were found nearly thirteen miles away near Kura Beach. The only body that was not near the main twenty-acre wreckage site was that of Julian Frank. His body was discovered near Snow's Marsh along the banks of the Cape Fear River, nearly sixteen miles from the main crash site. The autopsy of Julian Frank showed that his legs had literally been blow off and that many metal and wire fragments, like those found in a bomb, were imbedded in his arms and torso. Investigators also found traces of nitrates commonly used in explosives on one of his arms and manganese dioxide, a chemical found in dry cell batteries, on one of his hands.

It was later reported that the flames could be seen from town and lit up the early morning sky. When the fire department arrived at the scene shortly after sunrise, it was immediately obvious to them that there would be no survivors found in the twisted, smoldering wreckage. The gruesome task of putting out the remaining fires and recovering the bodies and remains of the victims was left to these gallant first responders. The remains of the passengers and crew were taken to a nearby high school in Southport for identification. The aircraft itself was taken to the Wilmington airport for reconstruction and a forensic study of the cause or causes of the crash.

The wreckage of National Airlines flight 2511
near Bolivia, North Carolina.

My uncle, Donald Kendall—Eddie's son-in-law and the chairman of Pepsi Cola—left New York City the next day and was tasked with the awful duty of identifying the admiral's remains. Don knew immediately which body was Eddie's, because his father-in-law always wore his 1912

Naval Academy class ring, a ring given to me by my mother when I graduated from college and one that I still wear to this day.

Interestingly enough, the cause of the National flight 2511 crash has never been conclusively determined. And even at this writing, more than sixty-two years later, the case and investigation of this doomed aircraft still remains open. One final note—my family never took our flight to Hobe Sound, Florida, and I was never to be introduced to my namesake, Admiral Edward Orrick McDonnell

CHAPTER ELEVEN

After the initial shock of Eddie McDonnell's tragic and sudden death abated, the family tried to continue on in a normal fashion. Although the final adoption was delayed for a week or so, due to my birth mother's indecision, eventually, it was finalized. Betty and Arthur Barry had finally become the parents of a rather large and homely baby boy. Several months later, we all moved to my father's new JAG posting in Heidelberg, Germany.

Donald Kendall went back to New York and continued doing an amazing job as the Chairman of PepsiCo. My Auntie Ann, now divorced from Don, was on the hunt for husband number three. Indeed, life did go on. Yet, in some ways, everything had changed. The family had lost its patriarch and anchor.

After Eddie's remains were identified by Don Kendall, his body was sent to a local mortuary and prepared for shipping back to the Washington, DC, area. The family had already decided to bury Eddie in "Admiral's Corner" at Arlington National Cemetery. Because of our impending move to Germany, the process was accelerated, and Eddie was buried with full military honors within a month or so of his death.

Another interesting fact that I uncovered during my research was the large number of newspapers that carried my grandfather's obituary. Newspapers from *The New York Times* and *The Wall Street*

Journal, to *The Washington Post* and *The San Francisco Examiner* carried the details of the crash and Eddie's demise.

Obviously, the possible bombing of a commercial airliner in the US was very big news. Yet, in nearly every report and news story, the only victim's name that was prominently mentioned was Vice Admiral Edward O. McDonnell's. Of course, they all mentioned Eddie's Medal of Honor and outstanding military career. But it was his second career as an investment banker and board member of Pan Am, United, Hertz, and PepsiCo that drew most of the attention. I guess it's big news story when a highly decorated war hero is killed tragically and suddenly. But it's a huge news story when that hero was an incredibly important and extremely successful millionaire Wall Street investment banker.

Adm. McDonnell

Obituary picture from the *New York Times*, 1960.

Another major change that confronted the family was Helen McDonnell's mental state. She had begun drinking heavily after the death of her son, Edward Jr., in North Africa during the early days of World War II. But Eddie had always been there to help control and comfort her, as well as reduced both the scale and the negative impact of that drinking.

Shortly after Eddie's death, Nana McDonnell went into a deep, dark, and extremely depressed state that was exacerbated by her excessive drinking and smoking. Her dramatic weight loss and chronic emphysema turned this normally active and social women into a frail and weak shadow of her former self.

My Auntie Ann and my oldest sister, Kathleen, had to make frequent trips to Nana's two residences to take her to the doctor or hospital while my father and our family were stationed overseas. She would occasionally be caught drinking and driving. This would lead to legal troubles and eventually to the loss of her driving privileges. She was resentful and blamed Eddie for his choice to take the second National Airlines flight. The deep depression and the accompanying mood swings caused by the loss of both men in her life never left my grandmother.

My earliest memories of my Nana McDonnell were of a small, wrinkled, old women who smelled of cigarette smoke and liquor. She would verbally abuse her household staff, frequently telling them that they were useless or accuse them of stealing and firing them on the spot. This would cause an immediate panic and force one of the family members to drop everything and rush to her side to reassure her maids, cooks, or secretaries that they were still needed and employed. These were just a few of the outward signs of a truly mean-spirited, spiteful, and bitter old women.

Yet, as my mother repeated frequently, this bitter old woman was not the person who had raised her and her brother and sister. This was not the loving mother and wife who she had grown up with. Nana had always taken great pride in being a mother and grandmother. Betty told stories of how her mother played with her and her siblings, as well as her grandchildren, when they were little. Hide-and-seek, card and board games, and swimming and traveling were the norm. The person I knew was the exact opposite of the person my mother described.

The woman I knew certainly didn't act like the person who had traveled the world and developed relationships with many of the most important and influential people of her generation. Prior to her husband's demise, Helen seemed to have relished and enjoyed her life, despite the premature death of her son.

Helen had exemplified what it meant to be a true Southern Belle. She displayed all the social graces, was an enjoyable companion and a welcoming and gracious hostess. Helen McDonnell, in a word, had been the perfect complement to Edward McDonnell. Now, after her husband's death, and without his steadying and calming influence, she had become resentful, demanding, and incredibly difficult to deal with.

I recall overhearing the occasional conversation between her and my mother. Their discussions would often revolve around her son Edward Jr. These conversations never seemed like happy memories, only sad ones. She would often lament that her husband should have done more to ensure her son's safety. Eddie should have demanded that "Boy" join the Navy. He should have never allowed him to join that "dreadful" Army Air Corps. After all, the Army had nothing but inferior aircraft and officers. If only Edward Jr. had joined the Navy, her husband Eddie, because of his rank, could have "magically" protected her only son.

This resentment went far beyond her husband. Helen also resented her daughters, their children, and especially my father, who she referred to by his last name, Barry. "I don't have much use for that West Pointer, Barry," she would say while baiting my mother during one of her many moody periods.

Betty would simply blame the alcohol. It was not unusual for Helen to drink nearly a full bottle of vodka daily. My grandmother was a mean and nasty drunk! Even as a young adult, my Nana had always enjoyed a good libation or two. But due to the nature off my grandfather's military and business standing, as well as his tremendous force of will, she had usually limited her drinking or only let loose in private.

All that changed after the events on the night of January 6, 1960. Moodiness and excessive drinking were normal daily occurrences. I don't recall how many times, after we returned to the United States, my mother would have to leave on a moment's notice and fly off to one of her mother's homes.

The shrubs and bushes around the Oyster Bay/Center Island and Hobe Sound homes were littered with empty and partially empty bottles of vodka, hidden from all and mostly forgotten by Helen. Betty was on a first name basis with the county sheriffs and local police. They were sometimes referred to as "The Black and White

Taxis," since they would often just load up Helen and bring her home after one of her binges.

Helen's maids were constantly accused of stealing her liquor, though they were simply hiding it per my mother's orders. This would trigger the inevitable drive, license or not, to the local liquor store, where Helen would often be found unconscious or incoherent in the parking lot. Sometimes she would be found walking home after losing her keys due to a few to many swigs.

Helenlost her driver's license privileges in both New York and Florida soon after Eddie's death. This was after several impaired driving incidents. Yet even this didn't deter her from these "booze cruise" drives. No, instead, we would get a midnight phone call from the Hobe Sound police, which would result in Betty's call to her lawyer, who, of course, would post bail and return Helen to her house.

The following mornings, after the realization of what she had done sunk in, instead of being contrite, she would demand the bottle she had purchased the previous evening. When no bottle was forthcoming, she would accuse her maids or cook of stealing it and, in a fit of rage, fire them on the spot. This was a steady routine that continued for many years.

It was also one of the more constant and vivid memories of my childhood—a late evening call, followed by a mad dash to Denver's Stapleton International Airport the next morning for the lengthy flight to New York or Florida, to hire back Helen's household staff and hopefully get there prior to her next liquor run and binge.

Occasionally during my summer vacation months or winter holidays, my mother would take me with her as her traveling companion. These surprise trips were truly one of the best benefits that I enjoyed as a child and young man.

We would arrive in New York City or West Palm Beach and travel by limo to one of Helen's homes. After clearing out the liquor, hiring back the long-suffering household staff, and resolving the rest of Helen's self-inflicted messes, Betty would plan on various escapes that would help ease the tensions.

These excursions often included visiting locations that held a special place in my mother's memories from childhood. Other times, we would visit an area or site that was significant to her father or her family in some other way.

These travel opportunities were always special to me. They would often expose me to the fine arts or other cultural events that children of my age were generally unaware of. These excursions would allow me to put faces and places onto the characters and locations that were so integral to my mother's stories. I was, in a way, through these visual connections, able to connect physically and emotionally with my grandfather and the stories that I so treasured.

The Hobe Sound house on Jupiter Island, Florida, 1968.

Visits to the beach house in Hobe Sound, Whiticar Boat Yard in Stuart, and NAS Pensacola in Florida brought me closer to the areas that were important to my grandfather. Flying into LaGuardia airport to visit my grandmother's house in Center Island would remind me of the importance of that airport in my grandfather's life. How many trips with Pan Am had started from that very spot on the north shore of Long Island?

Driving into Oyster Bay to buy groceries in my grandfather's Jaguar sedan with the dual gas tanks would almost always trigger one of my mother's favorite complaints. "How the hell are we supposed to go anywhere when none of us know how to switch the gas tanks on this damn car that gets such lousy mileage?"

Eating brunch at the Piping Rock Country Club or playing tennis on the same courts as my grandfather were more than just glimpses into his past. It almost seemed like I was reliving his past.

The Center Island house on Oyster Bay outside of Glenn Cove, New York, 1969.

Then there were the longer trips to catch a show on Broadway. Visiting FAO Schwarz, shopping at Macy's, and dining in the city were true adventures for a young child. Of course, we would stay at the Waldorf Towers where Eddie owned an apartment for many years. All of this gave me invaluable insights into the way my grandfather lived. Needless to say, he lived life exceedingly well!

THE SECRETARY OF THE NAVY
WASHINGTON

JUN 17

My dear Mrs. McDonnell:

It has been my pleasure to name the escort
ship DE-1043, EDWARD MCDONNELL, in honor of your
distinguished husband.

This fine new ship, an important addition to
our fleet, will be constructed at the Avondale
Shipyards, Inc., Westwego, Louisiana. The keel
was laid on 1 April 1963 and the launching is
scheduled for 7 December 1963.

It is a singular honor for me to invite you
to serve as sponsor to christen the EDWARD MCDONNELL.
The U.S. Navy Supervisor of Shipbuilding at that
plant will arrange with you the particular details
concerning the launching ceremony.

I sincerely hope that you will accept this invitation to participate in a tradition that has long
been cherished by the Navy.

Sincerely yours,

Fred Korth

Mrs. Edward McDonnell
Horse Shoe Road
Mill Neck, Long Island
New York

Letter informing the family of the naming of Destroyer Escort
DE-1043, 1963.

"Fortune favors the brave" was certainly true in the case of Eddie McDonnell. And because of his well-lived life, other opportunities and honors followed shortly after his death. We know he was given the rare privilege of a military funeral with full honors at Admiral's Corner in Arlington National Cemetery. The obituaries and stories that followed in papers throughout the country outlined this remarkable man and his legacy. Yet, in June of 1963, Eddie received one of his greatest accolades and honors.

Several months earlier, on April 1, 1963, the Navy laid the keel for a new destroyer escort at Avondale Shipyards in Louisiana. In a letter dated June 17, 1963, the secretary of the Navy invited my grandmother to serve as the sponsor at the christening of the DE-1043. He also announced that he was naming the ship in honor of Admiral E.O. McDonnell.

My mother Betty and grandmother Helen with two officials
at the christening of the DE-1043.

About nine months after receiving the secretary's letter, the "Eddie Mac," as the ship would be called during its years of service, was christened at the Avondale yard. The date was February 15, 1964. It was a cool, almost cold, drizzly day in Louisiana. Yet, promptly at 10:30 a.m., Helen Fisher McDonnell, escorted by my mother, swung the neatly bound bottle of champagne. It broke cleanly and with a loud thud against the bow of the new ship. This was the signal for the supports to be released, and the gray, not quite completed destroyer escort slid sideways and with a mighty splash into the murky, blue-greenish water of the bayou. As the ship righted itself and gently floated on the briny waters of the Louisiana coast, the Navy band played the "Star-Spangled Banner" in the background. It was truly a remarkable moment in our family's history.

DE-1043 just prior to christening at Avondale Shipyards, February 1964.

Newly christened E. O. McDonnell, DE-1043, February 1964.

One year later to the day of its christening, the US Navy commissioned its newest anti-submarine destroyer escort, the USS *Edward O. McDonnell*, DE-1043, at the US Naval base in Charleston, SC. A formal lunch was served at the base's officer's club after the commissioning ceremony. It was at this time that my mother and grandmother presented the ship's captain, Commander Daniel L. Banks Jr., with a portrait of Admiral E. O. McDonnell, as well as a sterling silver coffee and tea service for the onboard officers' mess. Betty and her mother were overcome with emotions, but thoroughly enjoyed the attention, as well as the festivities.

Commissioning

U. S. S. EDWARD McDONNELL
(DE-1043)

UNITED STATES NAVAL BASE
CHARLESTON, SOUTH CAROLINA

15 FEBRUARY 1965

My only encounter with the "Eddie Mac" came a little over four years later. On May 13, 1969, the USS *E.O. McDonnell* arrived in Palm Beach, Florida, from Guantanamo Bay, Cuba. The ship's crew of 204 enlisted men and sixteen officers had been training in Cuba for seven weeks and was returning to Charleston when it stopped in Palm Beach. My mother and I had made another emergency trip to care for Helen and to close up the Hobe Sound house for the hot summer months. Hobe Sound and Jupiter Island lay just north of Palm Beach, so we ordered a driver and car to take the three of us to visit the ship while she was in port. While the visit and VIP treatment on board was wonderful, the real treat came several days later, as the ship sailed north from Florida to South Carolina.

Some of our friends and family gathered on our Hobe Sound beach to watch the destroyer escort go by. As soon as it was parallel to the small group, the ship's main gun opened up and presented us with a twenty-one-gun salute. Even my crusty old uncle Bernie Lincolns wept quietly as the ship thundered by. That may have been the only time, other than when he caught a huge, trophy sailfish, that I ever saw my uncle Bernie with tears in his eyes.

The USS *E.O. McDonnell*, DE-1043, 1972.

My mother explained to me, as we stood there on the beach that day, that the *Edward O. McDonnell* was more than just another war ship. It was, she said, an outward symbol of a grateful nation to one of its great naval heroes. The people who saw the ship in future years would wonder who Eddie McDonnell was. They would want to know more about him and why he was honored in this manner.

Those who served aboard the DE-1043 would know Eddie's story and take pride in serving aboard a ship named after one of their own, an officer and naval hero. They would always remember his name and what it stood for.

The "Eddie Mac," DE-1043, under way in heavy seas, 1974.

But this is just one of the many legacies that Eddie left for the benefit of all. His contributions to military aviation made our country stronger and the world a much safer place. His contributions to commercial aviation made travel safer and faster for all. Our world is now easier to explore then at any point in its history. Our ability to connect face to face has helped to promote a better understanding of our cultural similarities, as well as our differences. Trade has been both enhanced and increased due to the speed and size of our commercial aircraft.

Because of his skills as an investment banker, more companies were funded, thereby creating more and better paying jobs. His rigid standards and strict moral compass helped to guide some of the most important corporate decisions of the twentieth century. Because of men like Eddie McDonnell, workplace safety, fair practices, and wages were put ahead of corporate greed and obscene profits.

Of course, he made an extremely comfortable living while doing this. But his contributions to charities, the arts, and education cannot be overlooked. It was because of his success that he was able to give so much back to society. As Betty was so fond of repeating, "To whom much is given, from them, much is owed."

But maybe Eddie's greatest legacy was his involvement in the conservation of our endangered species, wildlands, and waters. I know this sounds odd when you consider the amount of fish and game that Eddie harvested over the course of his life, but no one championed our wild places, animal habitats, and natural resources more than Eddie McDonnell. The lands, habitats, and endangered species that he and others like him helped preserve were critical in a time when most people didn't understand their importance or even know where they were located.

His conservation and preservation efforts in Africa, Asia, South America, and Alaska led to the establishment of thousands of acres of national parks, game preserves, and open habitats that benefitted not only the fish and animals but also the indigenous people.

Can we imagine a world without elephants, polar bears, and wild Atlantic salmon? That might have been our reality without the efforts of men like Teddy Roosevelt, William Holden, and Eddie McDonnell. Their determined efforts and the foresight to recognize the need where men, both native and visitor, can hunt and fish were truly inspired. These wild places were set aside then for the benefits of all. And they are even more important today. This is what I hope will be Eddie's greatest public legacy and what he is remembered for.

But what of his other legacies? The private ones. These are certainly important as well. But they are important to a much more limited group of people. Eddie's private legacy to his family in general, and to me in particular, were in many ways critical to our successes and helped make us the people we are.

When Eddie McDonnell was killed, he was an extremely wealthy man. Maybe not by today's billionaire standards, but he certainly would have been considered in the upper one percent in terms of net worth. His real estate holdings, stocks, bonds, personal art, antiques, and gun collections were worth millions. Again, his was indeed a life well lived!

After all his bequests to charities, foundations, and schools, Eddie was still able to leave his family in excellent financial shape. His generosity toward his wife, daughters, and grandchildren was tremendous.

As Betty would say quite frequently, "My father worked very hard so that I wouldn't have to."

Eddie's generosity enabled my mother, father, and my siblings to enjoy the finer things and niceties that most families could not. My father was a successful man. But being an Army officer and lawyer for the state was not exactly putting him on the road to riches.

It was my mother and her father's wealth that allowed us to live at a much higher standard than most. Beautiful homes in Cherry Hills Village, Colorado, as well as an incredible beach home in Hobe Sound, Florida, were just part of the McDonnell perks. Private schools, skiing, and vacations to Hawaii, Europe, and Mexico were also benefits that we enjoyed. We were privileged, but we were also taught to serve and be generous with the gifts that we had received.

But what were Eddie's greatest legacies to me?

That was an easy question for me to answer. Eddie's greatest legacies to me were his inspiring story, and Betty, the one person who could have told those stories to me. These stories were told to me over and over by Betty. Her incredible memory and ability to relate these tales to a young child and, years later, to her adult son were meant to teach, inspire, and instill a sense of pride and determination. These stories I have shared with you did all those things and more.

Other than my wife and children, no other person or persons has impacted me more or meant more to my life than Betty. Of course, most mothers play a critical and pivotal role in the lives of their children. They feed, nurture, teach, and guide us. They comfort us and help us to understand what unconditional love is. But Betty was more than this. She was my friend and my mentor. She was a truly adventurous person who led by example.

The adventurous spirit that made Eddie a naval hero, successful businessman, and a tremendous sportsman was most certainly bequeathed to my mother, his youngest daughter.

Betty was an excellent golfer and tennis player. She loved the outdoors and fishing. But these were only some of her tamer pursuits.

She loved skiing, hiking, and white water rafting, and was truly a world traveler. But there was one sport that came to symbolize my mother best of all. It was as an equestrian that she truly excelled. She loved the thrill of an early morning fox hunt. It was the English style, chasing a pack of hounds, jumping fences, and charging over hills in the ice and snow that got her blood flowing.

I know there will be many of you who view this sport as barbaric and out of touch. But nothing could be further from the truth. We "rode to the hounds" to chase, never hoping to kill our quarry. Instead of foxes, we hunted coyotes. Larger, stronger, faster, and cleverer than a fox, the coyote is an elusive target and extremely difficult to catch and even harder to kill. Often, we would go years without catching one. Certainly, it was much more sporting than just looking through a rifle scope and pulling the trigger.

Have no doubt, Betty, as well as her uncle John McDonnell and cousin "Bootsie" Hearst, loved English foxhunting.

Much of my young life was devoted to the care and preparation of our mounts or horses for the "hunt." This sport involves riding on the back of a fifteen-hundred-pound thoroughbred, galloping through all kinds of weather, while chasing a coyote with a large pack of English fox hounds. What a concept!

Our hunting territory was Lawrence C. Phipps' Highlands Ranch, a thirty-three-thousand-acre cattle ranch just south of Denver. Most of the members of Colorado's Arapahoe Hunt bore battle scars. Broken legs, arms, and even necks were commonplace. Betty broke her wrist in a nasty fall from her horse and hardly missed a beat. Less than two weeks later, she was back on her horse riding and controlling the beast with one wrist and hand in a cast.

My father had his hand stepped on and crushed by his horse's spiked shoe while attempting to jump a four-plus-foot fence on an icy and frozen Sunday morning. The three pins he had inserted into his right hand would be with him for the rest of his life. This was indeed a high-risk, high-reward endeavor. And these were the thrill-seeking parents who adopted me.

As I mentioned, I was born three weeks before Eddie was killed. I still have a difficult time imagining the feelings of ultimate joy mixed with pain and loss that my mother must have experienced during that time. I would never say that I was a replacement for Betty's father, but it's funny how a newborn infant can distract you from your thoughts and occupy your time like nothing else. No one could have replaced Eddie in my mother's heart. But the boundless amount of love she felt for him was at least in part transferred to me. How fortunate I was to have been welcomed into this remarkable family.

Several of the other remarkable talents that Betty possessed are certainly worth another mention. Her incredible memory was frequently the topic of conversation during the adult discussions involving my parents. My mother could remember a broken promise or a harsh word from decades ago. My father would often remark to us kids that we do not what to challenge one of my mother's memories, unless we wanted to be proven wrong and scorned for our foolishness.

Her other truly remarkable gift was the gift of gab. I mean, my mother could talk! Not the natural ramblings of someone lost in the past and trying to relive their own personal history. Her storytelling abilities rivaled the great tale-tellers from Ireland or Scotland. Her gift was the ability to turn even the most mundane and trivial tale into one that would be remembered for years. Betty's use of descriptive words, colorful phrases, and intimate details made her a welcomed guest and fascinating hostess at any event.

Some of my favorite times were spent around the backgammon board on a snowy day listening to Betty tell me another story of her father. It certainly didn't matter that I had heard the story many times before. There was usually a new detail or twist, like the type of rifle Eddie used during a particular bear hunt in Alaska. Or what he and his brother John had for dinner their first night in London or Paris. This was all important to me because it furthered my connection to Eddie and made me feel that I had indeed known him.

I loved the stories and thought about my grandfather all the time.

I would imagine myself at his side on fishing and hunting expeditions or as his tail gunner in a biplane over France. The haystack by the barn would become my plane or ship or be magically transformed into the roof of the Terminal Hotel in Vera Cruz. The pastures and fields around our home were transformed into the grasslands of Africa or the battlefields of Europe. A child's imagination can bring them into new worlds and different eras with the right subject and proper stimuli.

I have often asked myself, *What kind of childhood would I have experienced if Eddie had lived beyond age sixty-nine?* All but one of his siblings lived well into their eighties and were healthy and energetic until the end. It's conceivable that Eddie could have lived another fifteen or twenty years. That means that I could have benefitted from his advice, expertise, and guidance well into my teenage years.

Would I have turned out differently? Possibly. Would he have enjoyed my company, traveled with me, and included me on his many fishing and hunting adventures? I would certainly hope so. Would I have been inspired by his business acumen and learned some of his extraordinary business skills? The answers to these and other questions is that I'll never know.

Yet one of the greatest ironies is that I probably know as much about his life and his heroic deeds as any of my cousins or siblings. I think that is why I was chosen by Betty to tell the story of Eddie McDonnell. My mother recognized a need for me to learn about her father and then share his story. She wanted me to write down and remember these tales. She of all people knew that her father's story must be told, and I was the one to do it. She even went so far as to make me promise her, just months before her death, that I would tell his story.

This is why I am now sharing his remarkable story with the world. Yes, because of the promise, yet also because of the importance of the tale. Our world is going a bit crazy these days. Wars, the rewriting of our history, and false prophets predicting gloom and doom for everything from climate change to the end of our democracy. We need a reason to feel good about ourselves, our country, and our world.

In times of great strife and need, heroes must step up and answer the call. Great men and women must find a way to fix and heal our pain and suffering. They must fill whatever void needs to be filled. We must be inspired and realize that things can and will get better. That's the true reason for the book.

We can all answer the call and be the hero of our own story. We need to know that character and perseverance are necessary if we wish to succeed and leave our own legacy, one that hopefully inspires others to do better and effect the changes that are needed for our world to become a better place.

I now realize that, even though this remarkable man was taken from me on that dark, cold January night in 1960, his legacy is his story and the daughter he left behind to tell it. It is this legacy that I'm sure he would have wanted me to share with others to show anyone who is willing to listen—that anything is possible when you have a belief in your cause, the courage to try, and the will to succeed.

I am hoping to bring a sense of pride and a better understanding of Eddie's achievements to my family. There are multiple generations who don't know or understand the impact their great grandfather or great uncle had on both his family and the nation. They didn't have the benefit of Betty.

I am also hoping that, with the completion of this book, I too can find a sense of closure and let go of the resentment I have felt for most of my life. Why was I the only grandchild never to have met or known this man? Why couldn't I have shared in his love and enjoyed his company and sense of adventure? I think I know the answer finally after all these years.

Being a naturally curious person, I desperately wanted to know the man my mother talked so lovingly about. I needed to know his story and discover for myself what made this man so extraordinary. Why did my own mother love her father more than any other person in her life? There had to be something quite remarkable about this person.

Now, after spending the better part of three years researching, verifying, and writing the story of Eddie McDonnell, the answer I was looking for became quite clear. My purpose was to research and write about Eddie because it had to be done. We need heroes. We need examples of American exceptionalism. We need to understand that while none of us is perfect, some of us will always strive to reach our fullest potential, our own level of greatness, if you will. That is the story of Eddie McDonnell. That is why this story had to be told. That is one of the main reasons why I believe that I was destined to be adopted into this truly remarkable family.

Betty gave me the gifts of a mother's love. She gave me the stories to inspire me to achieve my own destiny. She gave me a purpose after she and my father were gone and my children were raised. "Write," she said. "Tell the world about your namesake and grandfather!"

So, that is what I've done. I wrote this book. After receiving so much from Betty, this is my final gift to her. And it was truly a gift from my heart and filled with the same love that I got from her.

So, thank you, Grandfather Eddie, for being a truly exceptional man. Thank you, Betty, for sharing the stories in such a way as to make me want to share them with the world. Thank you to my extended family for being so damn interesting. And thank you to Renee and my children, Ed, Howard, and Eva, for putting up with me, for supporting my endeavors, my obsessive behavior, and at times, my creative madness. And thank you to my readers for taking the time to learn about Admiral Eddie. This is his story, told, retold, written, and remembered. He was truly the greatest naval aviator in American history.

Promise kept!

Edward Orrick McDonnell

Do not allow the history of American exceptionalism to be fictionalized and distorted by those far less then exceptional!

CPSIA information can be obtained
at www.ICGtesting.com
Printed in the USA
JSHW021800031122
32551JS00006B/22